A CENTURY *of*
DERBY

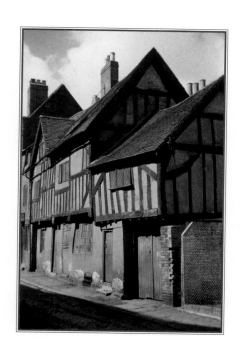

1971 This year saw the completion of the rebuilding of Derby Cathedral, a project first mooted in the 1930s when Sir Ninian Comper proposed a dome and transepts. It was only begun, to the designs of Sir Ninian's son Sebastian, under Provost Beddoes in 1968. James Gibbs's superb Baroque church was extended with a retro-choir and vestry, and with chapter room, choir school and offices beneath it. The effect, although derided by Modernists, was tactful and dignified, as is apparent from this sylvan view taken from the east side of St Mary's Bridge, with the tower of the silk mill on the right.

A CENTURY *of* DERBY

MAXWELL CRAVEN

SUTTON PUBLISHING

This book was first published in 2000 by Sutton Publishing Limited.

This new paperback edition first published in 2007 by
Sutton Publishing, an imprint of NPI Media Group
Cirencester Road · Chalford · Stroud · Gloucestershire · GL6 8PE

British Library Cataloguing in Publication Data
A catalogue record for this book is available from the British Library.

ISBN 978-0-7509-4911-8

Front endpaper: Saturday morning shoppers, bottom of St Peters Street, 1949.
Back endpaper: Derby Silk Mill, viewed from the Derwent, 1974.
Half title page: The Nottingham Castle inn, St Michaels' Lane, 1962. The inn had stood on this site since at
least 1550 and was demolished in 1964.
Title page: Corporation swimming baths, 1932. Aslin's powerful Classical Revival entrance, Queen Street, is
seen here shortly before completion.

To the members of the Derby Civic Society
for fighting so doughtily to preserve the
best of Derby from an ever-increasing tide
of philistinism

Typeset in Photina.
Typesetting and origination by
Sutton Publishing.
Printed and bound in England.

Derby's full armorial achievements, granted 1939.

Contents

1965 A pioneering move, actively promoted by the recently founded Derby Civic Society, was the pedestrianisation of Sadler Gate, the only medieval-width main road to have escaped widening in the city centre. Consequently, the buildings in it, including the Old Bell Hotel (see p. 50), are nearly all remarkably early, Georgian façades hiding a variety of earlier, gabled, buildings. One of the earliest, Eager's (to let, behind the ladder, right) was, in fact, never altered, and retains its late Tudor front to this day. The tall stone building to the left is the entrance to the Strand Arcade, built to designs by John Somes Story in 1879 and intended to emulate the Burlington Arcade in London, a hope never really fulfilled. In the background is the surviving 1610 tower of St Werburgh's Church.

Britain: A Century of Change

Two women encumbered with gas masks go about their daily tasks during the early days of the war. (*Hulton Getty Picture Collection*)

The sixty years ending in 1900 were a period of huge transformation for Britain. Railway stations, post-and-telegraph offices, police and fire stations, gasworks and gasometers, new livestock markets and covered markets, schools, churches, football grounds, hospitals and asylums, water pumping stations and sewerage plants totally altered the urban scene, and the country's population tripled with more than seven out of ten people being born in or moving to the towns. The century that followed, leading up to the Millennium's end in 2000, was to be a period of even greater change.

When Queen Victoria died in 1901, she was measured for her coffin by her grandson Kaiser Wilhelm, the London prostitutes put on black mourning and the blinds came down in the villas and terraces spreading out from the old town centres. These centres were reachable by train and tram, by the new bicycles and still newer motor cars, were connected by the new telephone, and lit by gas or even electricity. The shops may have been full of British-made cotton and woollen clothing but the grocers and butchers were selling cheap Danish bacon, Argentinian beef, Australasian mutton and tinned or dried fish and fruit from Canada, California and South Africa. Most of these goods were carried in British-built-and-crewed ships burning Welsh steam coal.

As the first decade moved on, the Open Spaces Act meant more parks, bowling greens and cricket pitches. The First World War transformed the place of women, as they took over many men's jobs. Its other legacies were the war memorials which joined the statues of Victorian worthies in main squares round the land. After 1918 death duties and higher taxation bit hard, and a quarter of England changed hands in the space of only a few years.

The multiple shop – the chain store – appeared in the high street: Sainsburys, Maypole, Lipton's, Home & Colonial, the Fifty Shilling Tailor, Burton, Boots, W.H. Smith. The shopper was spoilt for choice, attracted by the brash fascias and advertising hoardings for national brands like Bovril, Pears Soap, and Ovaltine. Many new buildings began to be seen, such as garages, motor showrooms, picture palaces (cinemas), 'palais de dance', and ribbons of 'semis' stretched along the roads and new bypasses and onto the new estates nudging the green belts.

During the 1920s cars became more reliable and sophisticated as well as commonplace, with developments like the electric self-starter making them easier for women to drive. Who wanted to turn a crank handle in the new short skirt? This was, indeed, the electric age as much as the motor era. Trolley buses, electric trams and trains extended mass transport and electric light replaced gas in the street and the home, which itself was groomed by the vacuum cleaner.

A major jolt to the march onward and upward was administered by the Great Depression of the early 1930s. The older British industries –

textiles, shipbuilding, iron, steel, coal – were already under pressure from foreign competition when this worldwide slump arrived. Luckily there were new diversions to alleviate the misery. The 'talkies' arrived in the cinemas; more and more radios and gramophones were to be found in people's homes; there were new women's magazines, with fashion, cookery tips and problem pages; football pools; the flying feats of women pilots like Amy Johnson; the Loch Ness Monster; cheap chocolate and the drama of Edward VIII's abdication.

Things were looking up again by 1936 and new light industry was booming in the Home Counties as factories struggled to keep up with the demand for radios, radiograms, cars and electronic goods, including the first television sets. The threat from Hitler's Germany meant rearmament, particularly of the airforce, which stimulated aircraft and aero engine firms. If you were lucky and lived in the south, there was good money to be earned. A semi-detached house cost £450, a Morris Cowley £150. People may have smoked like chimneys but life expectancy, since 1918, was up by 15 years while the birth rate had almost halved.

In some ways it is the little memories that seem to linger longest from the Second World War: the kerbs painted white to show up in the

A W.H. Smith shop front in Beaconsfield, 1922.

blackout, the rattle of ack-ack shrapnel on roof tiles, sparrows killed by bomb blast. The biggest damage, apart from London, was in the south-west (Plymouth, Bristol) and the Midlands (Coventry, Birmingham). Postwar reconstruction was rooted in the Beveridge Report which set out the expectations for the Welfare State. This, together with the nationalisation of the Bank of England, coal, gas, electricity and the railways, formed the programme of the Labour government in 1945.

Times were hard in the late 1940s, with rationing even more stringent than during the war. Yet this was, as has been said, 'an innocent and well-behaved era'. The first let-up came in 1951 with the Festival of Britain and there was another fillip in 1953 from the Coronation, which incidentally gave a huge boost to the spread of TV. By 1954 leisure motoring had been resumed but the Comet – Britain's best hope for taking on the American aviation industry – suffered a series of mysterious crashes. The Suez debacle of 1956 was followed by an acceleration in the withdrawal from Empire, which had begun in 1947 with the Independence of India. Consumerism was truly born with the advent of commercial TV and most homes soon boasted washing machines, fridges, electric irons and fires.

Children collecting aluminium to help the war effort, London, 1940s. (*IWM*)

A street party to celebrate the Queen's Coronation, June 1953. (*Hulton Getty Picture Collection*)

The *Lady Chatterley* obscenity trial in 1960 was something of a straw in the wind for what was to follow in that decade. A collective loss of inhibition seemed to sweep the land, as the Beatles and the Rolling Stones transformed popular music, and retailing, cinema and the theatre were revolutionised. Designers, hairdressers, photographers and models moved into places vacated by an Establishment put to flight by the new breed of satirists spawned by *Beyond the Fringe* and *Private Eye*.

In the 1970s Britain seems to have suffered a prolonged hangover after the excesses of the previous decade. Ulster, inflation and union troubles were not made up for by entry into the EEC, North Sea Oil, Women's

Lib or, indeed, Punk Rock. Mrs Thatcher applied the corrective in the 1980s, as the country moved more and more from its old manufacturing base over to providing services, consulting, advertising, and expertise in the 'invisible' market of high finance or in IT.

The post-1945 townscape has seen changes to match those in the worlds of work, entertainment and politics. In 1952 the Clean Air Act served notice on smogs and pea-souper fogs, smuts and blackened buildings, forcing people to stop burning coal and go over to smokeless sources of heat and energy. In the same decade some of the best urban building took place in the 'new towns' like Basildon, Crawley, Stevenage and Harlow. Elsewhere open warfare was declared on slums and what was labelled inadequate, cramped, back-to-back, two-up, two-down, housing. The new 'machine for living in' was a flat in a high-rise block. The architects and planners who promoted these were in league with the traffic engineers, determined to keep the motor car moving whatever the price in multi-storey car parks, meters, traffic wardens and ring roads. The old pollutant, coal smoke, was replaced by petrol and diesel exhaust, and traffic noise.

Punk rockers demonstrate their anarchic style during the 1970s. (*Barnaby's Picture Library*)

Fast food was no longer only a pork pie in a pub or fish-and-chips. There were Indian curry houses, Chinese take-aways and American-style hamburgers, while the drinker could get away from beer in a wine bar. Under the impact of television the big Gaumonts and Odeons closed or were rebuilt as multi-screen cinemas, while the palais de dance gave way to discos and clubs.

From the late 1960s the introduction of listed buildings and conservation areas, together with the growth of preservation societies, put a brake on 'comprehensive redevelopment'. The end of the century and the start of the Third Millennium see new challenges to the health of towns and the wellbeing of the nine out of ten people who now live urban lives. The fight is on to prevent town centres from dying, as patterns of housing and shopping change, and edge-of-town supermarkets exercise the attractions of one-stop shopping. But as banks and department stores close, following the haberdashers, greengrocers, butchers and ironmongers, there are signs of new growth such as farmers' markets, and corner stores acting as pick-up points where customers collect shopping ordered on-line from web sites.

Millennium celebrations over the Thames
at Westminster, New Year's Eve, 1999.
(*Barnaby's Picture Library*)

Futurologists tell us that we are in stage two of the consumer revolution: a shift from mass consumption to mass customisation driven by a
desire to have things that fit us and our particular lifestyle exactly, and
for better service. This must offer hope for small city-centre shop
premises, as must the continued attraction of physical shopping,
browsing and being part of a crowd: in a word, 'shoppertainment'.
Another hopeful trend for towns is the growth in the number of young
people postponing marriage and looking to live independently, alone,
where there is a buzz, in 'swinging single cities'. Theirs is a 'flats-and-
cafés' lifestyle, in contrast to the 'family suburbs', and certainly fits in
with government's aim of building 60 per cent of the huge amount of
new housing needed on 'brown' sites, recycled urban land. There looks
to be plenty of life in the British town yet.

Derby: An Introduction

There was a time, about the middle of the twentieth century, when people thought of Derby as a centre of railway engineering and as the home of Rolls-Royce; if pressed, they might have added Royal Crown Derby, the eminent porcelain manufacturer. Today, although all three elements remain, albeit in changed form, the city has altered considerably. That transmutation has been all the more startling when contrasted with the situation in 1901, when Rolls-Royce had not yet been founded, and the population of what was then a newly created county borough (1888) stood at a relatively modest 105,912, in contrast to today's figure of almost a quarter of a million.

Derby was founded in the tenth century around a minster church, which had been built some time before the Viking incursions into the area in 874. A second minster church, dedicated to All Saints (since 1927 Derby Cathedral), was then founded and endowed with three outlying settlements, one of which contained the vestiges of Roman *Derventio*, the walls of which had acted as a fortified centre for the local Viking administration.

Derby's first charter dates back to *c.* 1155 and, despite the dominance of no fewer than six monastic institutions, expanded into a flourishing market town, grown prosperous on the produce of a hinterland dominated by modest but opulent landed estates rich in sheep, coal and lead. Their proprietors consequently built town houses in the borough, and spent money there, thus further enriching the burgesses. Indeed, by the early years of the eighteenth century Daniel Defoe was able to write of Derby as: 'A fine, beautiful and pleasant town; it has more families of gentlemen in it than is usual . . . and therefore here is a great deal of good and some gay company.'

By the 1780s, an enlightened coterie of men of science and industrial flair, which included Dr Erasmus Darwin FRS (grandfather and inspirer of Charles), John Whitehurst FRS and Jedediah Strutt, came to dominate the town. This group's links to the Lunar Society of Birmingham made Derby pre-eminent among provincial cities (Birmingham excepted) as a cradle of the industrial revolution.

Even when the town's first iron foundries were established from the 1790s they made architectural ornaments for the embellishment of the better houses of the region rather than workaday items. However, the establishment in 1784 of James Fox & Co., Britain's first precision

The Robert Adam interior of Derby's Georgian Assembly Rooms. They were damaged by fire and demolished in 1963.

machine tool makers, with Lunar Society support, heralded a change in Derby's industrial emphasis. There followed other engineering works and with the coming of the railway in 1839/40 (from 1844 the Midland Railway) this aspect burgeoned, so that by the beginning of the twentieth century the town was dominated by heavy engineering.

By 1901 Derby had benefited from forty years of street widening, and could boast many new commercial buildings, two railway lines – the Midland and the Great Northern Railway – and a tramway network of some twenty-one years' standing. The predominantly working population was concentrated to the south and south-east of the Midland Railway's station, in the still-expanding suburbs of New Normanton, Peartree and Litchurch. To the west lay a development of tape mills and silk mills interspersed with generally poor-quality early nineteenth-century artisans' housing gathered along the course of the Markeaton Brook.

In the south-eastern part of Derby were gathered numerous iron foundries (and one major brass foundry). Many had sprung up to supply components to the railway, which had encouraged the boom by founding a works. Streets of workers' housing grew up around these concentrations of heavy industry, with a scattering of corner pubs, off-licences and shops. The latter category included a large number of branches of the Derby Co-operative Society, founded in 1850 (and only the third in Britain).

Rolls-Royce relocated from Manchester in 1907, attracted by the low electricity prices and the availability of cheap land. At the time it was regarded as just another foundry. They manufactured prestige motor cars until 1946, when the facility moved to Crewe in Cheshire, and from 1914 aero engines were also produced, the triumphant result of the Hon. Charles Rolls's passion for aviation (not shared by his co-founder), buoyed up by the demands of the First World War. Thus, up to 1946, this company represented both strands of Derby's manufacturing base: 'luxury' market goods and heavy foundry-based engineering. After bankruptcy and nationalisation in 1971, Rolls-Royce remains the prime manufacturing industry in Derby.

Conversely, the amalgamation of the railways in 1923 and their nationalisation in 1948 led ultimately to the decline of locomotive and of rolling stock production. However, by the end of the twentieth century the railways were back in private hands, enormously slimmed down, and ultimately – it would appear – once again successful.

Into this gap came a mass of technologically based companies and, latterly, firms based on the information technology revolution. This had far-reaching demographic effects on the borough, itself given the status of a city in 1977. This came just three years after it was deprived of its autonomy under the 1974 Local Government Act, a state of affairs only reversed (to general relief) in 1996. Another major political change came in 1959 when Derby's status as the county town was lost to Matlock.

In order to accommodate its ever-increasing population, Derby was obliged to expand. In 1901, 1927 and 1968 major boundary revisions brought in more former villages, and by the end of the twentieth century most had been 'suburbanised'. From 1919 the open land between these villages was filled with municipal housing, while the boundary revision of 1927 had cleared the way for the building (in 1928) of a ring-road.

Transport changes reflected these trends. The tramways were electrified from 1904 and were replaced by trolleybuses from 1932. These succumbed to the motor bus in 1967. Likewise, railway provision receded with the closure of the former Great Northern Railway's western extension in 1967, and of the former Midland main line from Derby to Manchester via Buxton a year later. Indeed, services seemed to decline generally until, for the first time in over thirty years, there is once again a through London–Matlock service, and moves are afoot to re-open the line to Buxton.

In 1964 the Teacher Training College, founded in 1851, began to expand rapidly and became part of the Technical College in the 1970s. It was elevated to the status of a university in 1992, a change that brought a massive increase in the student population and resulted in the construction of new halls of residence, mainly in the old West End, itself cleared of low-quality nineteenth-century housing in the 1960s and '70s.

All these changes have been reflected in the ancient centre of the city, which still retains its basic medieval street layout. Until 1932 the banks of the River Derwent were crowded with various ugly developments that had been crammed on to the gardens of former gentry town houses. In that year, however, a Central Improvement Plan swept all this away and replaced it with a single wide boulevard running parallel to the river from Cockpit Hill to Queen Street.

A further scheme in 1971 saw the clearance of early nineteenth-century housing between Cockpit Hill and London Road to make way for a vast and particularly ugly shopping complex called the Eagle Centre. So poor was this that it had to be rebuilt in 1989–90, and is again at the time of writing (2000). Another concurrent scheme was to replace the 1764 Assembly Rooms, and its matchless Robert Adam interior. Except for the handsome Palladian façade, this splendid building was preremptorily destroyed. The new complex, designed by Sir Hugh Casson, and a monument to the 'Brutalist' School of Modernism, was completed at the expense of the whole of the northern side of the ancient Market Place. The façade of the old Assembly Rooms found no place in Sir Hugh's designs and was taken to Crich Tramway Museum, where it was re-erected.

Another destructive scheme was the building, from 1967, of the inner ring-road, which cost the city St Alkmund's Church, its only Georgian square, Herbert Spencer's birthplace and the setting of the Grade I listed St Helen's House of 1767. This plan was never fully completed, which saved Friar Gate, one of the region's premier urban conservation areas.

Another scheme in the 1990s involved a vast area between the Derwent and the line of the old canal, and an area immediately south of the former railway works, which was designated a special planning zone, optimistically named Pride Park. After a very slow start it began to fulfill its promise as the century closed. Perhaps the key element that eventually sparked development on Pride Park was the transfer to the site of the Derby County Football Club in 1997.

Although many of the heavy industries founded in the nineteenth century have gone, they have been survived, ironically, by two of the 'luxury' industries, which still flourish: clockmaking and porcelain manufacture. John Smith & Sons is a clockmaking firm founded by an ex-employee of the third (and last) John Whitehurst in 1850. Royal Crown Derby was founded in 1876 and took over the King Street China Factory – the 1848 successor to the original Crown Derby company – in 1935, giving them a genuine reason to celebrate their 250th anniversary as the century closed. The firm capped this by regaining its independence for the first time in decades through a successful management buy-out in June 2000 – a fitting coda to a century of fundamental change.

In conclusion, it is fair to observe that, despite much tragic environmental destruction, Derby retains more of its Georgian and earlier buildings than any other manufacturing town of comparable size. Being always just a little behind the times with current architectural trends, it enjoys a skyline blessedly free of high-rise blocks. The problem at the commencement of the twenty-first century is not so much the destruction of historic buildings but the poor quality of most new buildings, especially where locally based developers are involved.

This book aims to record at least some of the essential changes to the appearance and life of the city through the twentieth century. Readers must judge for themselves whether Derby has managed to retain its essential ambience and whether the *genius loci* of this much under-rated city remains intact.

The Start of the Century

1901 Late afternoon in Derby Market Place, with the market stallholders packing up for the day. All the transport, including the tram (far right), is horse-drawn, and the most recent building is the Royal Oak Inn, represented by the gable on the left, erected in Arts-and-Crafts style in 1890 and closed in 1916. The Guildhall was built after its predecessor was destroyed in a fire in 1841; it was designed by Henry Duesbury, grandson of the founder of the Derby China Factory.

1903 Opening to the north off the Market Place is Iron Gate, widened in 1866, with All Saints' Church tower – the second highest parish church tower in England after Boston Stump – rising beyond. Left is Crompton & Evans' Union Bank, later the Natwest, designed by J.A. Chatwin of Birmingham in Italian Palazzo revival style in 1880 and sensitively converted into a pub called the Standing Order in 1995. The Georgian building beyond was similarly transformed into a Yates's Wine Lodge in 1997. The street was pedestrianised in 1992.

1906 Running south from the Market Place is Cornmarket, funnelling out to accommodate the grain market that was held there until 1861. By 1906 the tramways had been electrified, although the cab-rank (foreground) shows that the horse still reigned supreme in that department. The Guildhall tower can be seen rising above the Palladian façade of the former town house of the Dukes of Devonshire of 1755, of which about two-thirds was demolished (together with all the buildings to the right) to make way for a Littlewood's store in 1969. Note the new timbered façade of the Old Angel Inn, replacing a late medieval predecessor.

1906 Opposite the Old Angel Inn was the Rose & Crown Inn, at this date run by Ernest Walton. It was part of the estate of the Liversage Trust, Derby's richest charity, founded by the will of prosperous dyer Robert Liversage in 1529. The gates, made by Derby ironsmith Edwin Haslam (1843–1913), bear ornate lead plaques to this effect. Haslam was the last in an unbroken succession of ornamental ironsmiths going back to Robert Bakewell (1682–1752), who made the ornate iron lamp overthrow just visible beyond the gates. It is now in store at Derby Museum.

19

1906 Albert Street, created by culverting the Markeaton Brook in 1848, is not a thoroughfare one would choose to stroll about today! In this autumn afternoon shot, traffic is virtually non-existent, bar a dray belonging to soft drinks manufacturers Burrows & Sturgess. The domed building is the 1861 Corn Exchange by Benjamin Wilson, which had been converted by this time into a variety theatre. On the left are the Central Vaults Inn and Simpson's printers in a range of 1864 by Giles & Brookhouse, who built most of Derby's commercial buildings in the town centre.

1902 St Peter's Street, a continuation of Cornmarket southwards across the culverted brook, takes its name from Derby's only city centre church (left) with surviving medieval fabric. The Midland Drapery had been founded twenty years before by Sir Edwin Ann and at this time the business was still expanding. The Georgian buildings to the right were replaced in 1912 by a stunningly exuberant Arts-and-Crafts branch of Boot's, happily still extant. The Midland Drapery was closed and demolished in the early 1970s.

20

1902 London Road runs from the southern end of St Peter's Street, and was once very rural. One of the earliest buildings erected in it, in 1814, was this Swedenborgian Chapel. It was demolished in 1902, but sadly no satisfactory photographic record of it has survived. Two rival congregations of the Swedenborgians managed to erect two chapels at this period. The demise of this one was the result of their later amalgamation. The sect has always been strong in Derby.

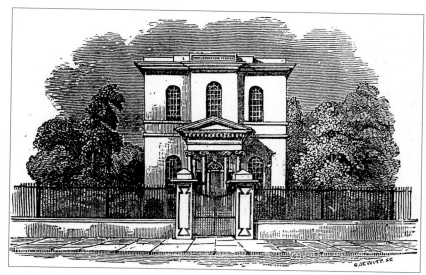

1906 Derby (Midland) Station was barely ten years old in the form seen here, having been extensively rebuilt for the second time in its history in 1895–7 by Charles Cope Trubshaw, the company's architect. It survived until 1984 when British Rail destroyed the entire edifice – including Francis Thompson's original 1839 Trijunct station, until then virtually intact behind the later accretions – and replaced it with what Professor Gavin Stamp has described as a 'hi-tech shack'. This view, with its newly introduced electric tramcars, was taken from the lower end of Station Street, by then renamed Midland Road.

1909 Cheapside seen from The Strand. The crowd, armed with banners, mark the installation at St Werburgh's Church (the tower of which is visible to the right) of the Rt Revd C.T. Abraham as the second suffragan Bishop of Derby. Cheapside was created from St Werburgh's churchyard in the early nineteenth century, and for many years it had a cab rank – note the cabbies' rest, examples of which these days survive only in London. All the buildings survive except the one at the extreme left, which was replaced by an extension to Derby Museum in 1964.

1905 Just outside the commercial centre of the town is Macklin Street, formerly Crosslanes, which connected Abbey Street with Green Lane and marked the southern limit of the gardens of the townhouses on the south side of The Wardwick. The buildings all date from around 1830. The narrow street to the left, beyond the brewer's dray which is delivering to Albert Walkerdine's grocery and off-licence, is Becket Well Lane. This side was hideously redeveloped with the failed Duckworth Square shopping centre and multi-storey car park in 1964, now due to be replaced again. On the right the spherical lamp marks the premises of the Friendly Societies' Medical Association. The large house in the far distance is Dr Sims's house of 1820, demolished for shops in 1924.

***c.* 1901** Uttoxeter New Road was pitched in 1819 and became an elegant late Regency suburban thoroughfare. In 1851 the Ladies' (teacher) Training College was erected under the aegis of the Diocese of Lichfield, and designed by Henry Isaac Stevens of Derby (1806–73). Expanding numbers led to its rebuilding – mainly the portion seen to the right – by Percy Heylin Currey FRIBA (1864–1942), an Arts-and-Crafts architect of considerable accomplishment, in 1895–1900. The college later became Derby Training College and in 1964 the Bishop Lonsdale College, before amalgamation with the technical college a decade later; this building became redundant in the early 1980s. It was saved from demolition for road-widening by spot-listing, and is now the College Business Centre.

***c.* 1901** As part of his additions to the training college, Currey designed this delightful chapel, completed in 1900. Because of the way the land fell away from the street level, it was built over a lecture hall. It was deconsecrated and cleared in the 1970s.

23

1901 London Road, looking south-east. The gradual break-up of the Osmaston Hall estate after it was bought by the Midland Railway in 1888 led to the release of land on either side of the road here, where grew up a small enclave of houses with shops, a Board School, chapel and inn. The development was called Wilmorton, after the Wilmot-Horton family, previous owners of the estate. In this Richard Keene Ltd view, the newspaper boards announce 'The Men who have Fought for the new Earl Roberts sift the Wheat from the Chaff'. Earl Roberts of Kandahar was so created in February 1901, at the height of the Boer War.

1901 London Road again, this time slightly further south, from the bridge over the Derby Canal immediately south of Wilmorton looking towards another new suburb, Crewton. This had been founded in the 1880s at the northern extremity of the parish of Alvaston as Newtown, but was renamed Crewton (after the Harpur-Crewe family of Calke Abbey, who owned the land) when it was absorbed by the county borough of Derby in 1901. Twelve years after this photograph was taken, the land to the left beyond the bridge was turned into Alvaston Park and embellished with a Carnegie Library (demolished in 1978). On the opposite side of the road, down which tramlines were laid in 1905, there is now a motor dealership.

1908   A contemplative moment by the Florentine boar in Derby Arboretum. The arboretum, to the south of Osmaston Road, was laid out for Joseph Strutt (third son of Jedediah) in 1840 by John Claudius Loudon, and was arguably Britain's first public park. At the time of the photograph it had reached its apogee; later industrial pollution, 'Digging for Victory' and vandalism ruined it. The boar was a free copy of the marble original, made around 1810 by William John Coffee, a former modeller at the China Factory, who later found fame in the USA. Disfigured by acid rain, it was destroyed by shrapnel when the adjacent Victorian bandstand received a direct hit from a German bomb in the Second World War; it was replaced by a bronze replica in 2006.

1909   Littleover Hollow. Until 1928 most of the (then) attractive village of Littleover, to the south-west of Derby, still lay outside the boundary. This street – painted by numerous local artists in the previous century – was a former hollow lane bounding the edge of the parkland of Littleover Old Hall, to the left in the picture. This was, unfortunately, 'developed' from the 1970s, diminishing its bucolic charms considerably. The timber-framed fifteenth-century cottage (right) survives, albeit much restored and made 'black-and-white'. Today the street is no wider, but the pony and trap, small dog and pedestrian would be in serious danger from the constant motor traffic.

25

1903 In the Edwardian period the birthplaces of most of Derby's famous sons could be visited, including that of the philosopher and sociologist Herbert Spencer (1824–1903) in Exeter Street on the east side of the Derwent where a Regency suburb grew up on an area formerly known as Canary Island. The plaque over the door was put up in the year the great man died, and was duly photographed. The area was eventually cleared from 1966 to make way for the inner ring-road. A similar fate befell Spencer's later home in Wilmot Street – a poor way to honour one of the nineteenth century's greatest philosophers.

1902 Increasing prosperity led to the development of Duffield Road as a well-to-do-suburb from the 1850s. This (recent) photograph shows one of the few twentieth-century domestic buildings to reach the Statutory List: Austwick (114 Duffield Road) was designed by the local partnership of Barry Parker & Sir Raymond Unwin in 1902–3 in innovative Arts-and-Crafts style. Once the main route from Derby to the north, Duffield Road originated as a turnpike in 1756, but by 1900 had acquired raised pavements embellished with locally cast iron bollards linked by chains, just visible in the foreground. It is now a conservation area.

c. **1908**   Derby racecourse was established on low-lying ground north of Nottingham Road to the east of Derby in the 1840s, the previous course having been taken over to build the railway station. In 1852 Henry Duesbury – designer of the Guildhall – built this splendid new grandstand, but by the date of this postcard it had become too small and was replaced in 1911. Unfortunately, despite the course's success, the rather puritanical borough council decided not to revive racing after the Second World War, turning it instead into a playing field. The final race on the card of the last meeting, held on 2 September 1939, was won by (Sir) Gordon Richards.

1900   One of the first new buildings of the Edwardian era was the Friendly Societies and Trades Union Hall in Burton Road, designed by Alexander MacPherson, who prepared this perspective view for his clients in 1900. It was completed in 1907, but was demolished, after having declined into a form of hostel, in the 1980s. Attempts to save it by Derby Civic Society met with little support from either the Friendly Societies or the Trades' Union fraternities, despite its central role in Derby's twentieth-century labour history. The site is now occupied by a doctors' surgery and pharmacy.

1902 Standing in Ashbourne Road near Windmill Hill Lane, where its route to the town centre commenced, is original Derby Tramways Co. horse car no. 22. The company had started operations in 1880 and had been taken over by the Corporation from 1 November 1899. The system was converted to electric traction between 1904 and 1907. Behind the vehicle is some of the parkland of Markeaton Hall, now the site of the relocated Royal School for the Deaf.

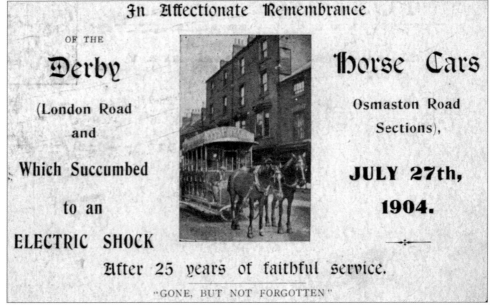

In Affectionate Remembrance

OF THE

Derby

(London Road

and

Which Succumbed

to an

ELECTRIC SHOCK

horse Cars

Osmaston Road

Sections),

JULY 27th,

1904.

After 25 years of faithful service.

"GONE, BUT NOT FORGOTTEN"

1904 Not everyone, it seems, was in favour of the introduction of electric trams in 1904. This satirical card marks the transition on the first route to be affected – London and Osmaston roads – as from 27 July 1904. Car no. 8 is depicted on the latter.

28

1904   One of Derby's most famous sons was the 1st Lord Curzon, later Marquess Curzon of Kedleston. Although this eminent Tory politician's family home, Kedleston Hall, lay just outside the borough, the Curzons had a long association with the town; they owned a certain amount of land in the central area and for a long time had had a town house there. George Nathaniel Curzon (1859–1925) served as Viceroy of India from 1898 to 1904, was Lord Privy Seal (1915–16), Lord President of the Council and Leader of the Lords (1916–19 and 1924–5), dying shortly after losing the race for the prime ministership to Stanley Baldwin. On 28 July 1904, on his triumphal return from India, he was made an Honorary Freeman of the Borough, receiving a fine ormolu-mounted Royal Crown Derby casket with his certificate, as seen here.

"THE GOLD CASKET & SCROLL"
PRESENTED TO
LORD CURZON
DERBY 28TH JULY 1904

820

1908   A lesser light was George Henry Bassano (1840–1913). Of north Italian stock, one of his ancestors had been 'head-hunted' by Henry VIII to join the band of the king's musicians at court, and their descendants had served in this capacity until banished to Lichfield at the outbreak of the Civil War. A member of the family came to Derby in the eighteenth century as an attorney. They also produced a fine local painter, Francis, and an international diva, Louisa. George Henry was a manufacturing electrician. Having decided that the phonographs and early gramophones he had seen were of insufficient quality, he produced the Rolls-Royce of such machines, the 'Bassanophone', from 1907. This superb 1908 example of these very rare devices – they sold only slowly, being extremely expensive – was acquired for Derby Museum in 1991.

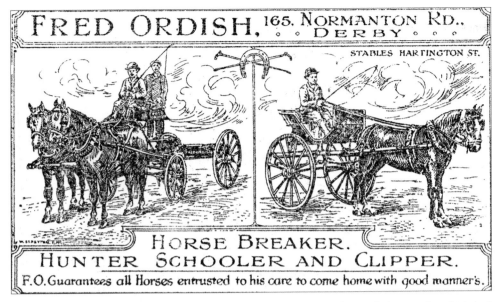

1903 Fred Ordish, who died in this year, was a typical practitioner of one of those trades which had flourished in the days when Derby was a county town and a centre of excellence for the local gentry. His business was carried on by his widow Annie for many years. There was a good saddlery in Derby – appropriately enough in Sadler Gate – until the early 1990s. Today this sort of trade has to be sought out in places like Bakewell or Ashbourne.

1906 Sir Herbert Raphael was a London barrister from a prominent banking family who was the 'carpetbagging' Liberal MP for South Derbyshire elected in the 1906 Liberal landslide. He is seen here (standing, left) at a party rally at the Derby Drill Hall handing out a large silver trophy wrought in the style of the Warwick Vase. He received a baronetcy in 1911, and lost his seat at the 1918 'Coupon' election. He lived as tenant at Allestree Hall – the only major country house within the present boundaries of the city still standing – until his death in 1924.

The First World War Era

1911 The Spot on 5 August, photographed by Charles Barrow Keane for the borough surveyor. The Spot is that point, at the southern (upper) end of St Peter's Street, where the London Road (left) and Osmaston Road (right) diverge. The former is an eighteenth-century turnpike; previously London traffic went via Osmaston Road and Swarkestone Bridge. The statue of Queen Victoria by Charles Bell Birch was unveiled on 28 June 1906 by King Edward VII on his visit to the Royal Agricultural Show, then held in the grounds of Osmaston Hall, nearby. It was removed to the grounds of the Derbyshire Royal Infirmary (where it still stands) in 1925 because it was too heavy for the public lavatories built beneath it!

1911 Derby was considered dilatory by central government in not undertaking the clearance of slum properties quickly enough, although in truth there were comparatively few true slums compared to the situation in, say, Nottingham. These houses, however, were cleared in 1911–12 from Summer Hill, off Becket Well Lane, just south of Victoria Street (see p. 22) and date from the late eighteenth century. They were built very small and to an atrocious standard.

1911 The upper room of one of the Summer Hill houses, photographed by the inspectors in 1911; conditions are clearly appalling, and damp is rampant. The area was dominated by at least two tinsmithing concerns, and at the time of writing is about to be redeveloped.

1912 Derby had two main stations, Midland (MR) and Friar Gate (GNR), but it was also served by trains of the North Staffordshire Railway which connected the Midland station with Stoke-on-Trent. In this view NSR 0–6–2T no. 1 leaves Derby with an all-stations train to the potteries capital.

1913 Rolls-Royce commenced making their unique motor cars at their new works on Nightingale Road in 1907, and rapidly expanded, drawing on a skilled workforce and attracting new workers from outside. They were benevolent employers, and this view celebrates their annual Field Day – works outings and family sports – held on 12 July that year. The advent of aero engine construction early in the First World War set off further expansion which led to the modification and eventual abandonment of these amiable events in the postwar period.

1913 Another sunny July day, and Mr Charles Spalton, proprietor of an agricultural meal manufacturing business on Ashbourne Road, drives up Friar Gate – then as now Derby's finest Georgian street – to his works in his pony and trap. The bridge in the distance, a fine ornate structure by Andrew Handyside & Co. of Derby of 1876, carries the GNR. The tower, right, marks the colossal Royal School for the Deaf (see page 97). The left-hand side, built up from 1768, has hardly changed, however.

1913 Although the beast and grain markets were dispatched from the open streets in the 1860s, stalls still thronged the Market Place, The Morledge, and Cockpit Hill at the turn of the century. The Morledge was the setting for the annual Easter Fair, seen here in 1913, and so continued until municipal tidy-mindedness banished it to distant Alvaston in 1924. It was not until 1948 that fairs returned to the city centre, when they were held on the site of Michael Thomas Bass's open air baths, decommissioned after the Second World War. By 1913 the fairs, originally focused on trading, had degenerated into fun fairs accompanied by a form of flea market, as evidenced by the stalls in the foreground. The large chimney on the left is Derby's famous shot-tower, built with Cox's lead works in 1809 and demolished in 1932. To the right is the colour works of Messrs Pegg & Ellam Jones.

1912 The campaign of street widening that began in 1866 continued sporadically until the 1920s, when Queen Street, seen here, looking south towards the tower of All Saints' (from 1927 the Cathedral), was finally dealt with, with the loss of all the Georgian buildings to the right. The street opening, left, is the top of Full Street, widened in 1944 and again in the 1960s. At its corner is a timber-framed inn, the Old Dolphin, which was allegedly founded in 1530, and recorded in the earlier seventeenth century, from which era the fabric certainly dates.

1914 The Wardwick, another of Derby's finest streets, was widened in 1914, and the three grand town houses on the north side, seen here, were pulled down for that purpose in July that year. All had long since been shop-fronted. The one nearest the camera was built for Dr Francis Fox in 1784 using mouldings bought in the sale of the stock from the yard of builder-architect Joseph Pickford (1734–82). It was later the birthplace of Sir Charles Fox, engineer of the Crystal Palace. The effect of the demolition was to create a garden beside the museum, an extension of which in 1964 created the present Museum Square.

35

1916 Derby School was founded in 1554–5 and moved in 1863 to Joseph Pickford's splendid Palladian mansion, St Helen's House, where it remained until the beginning of the 1970s when, 'comprehensivised', it migrated to the outskirts of Littleover. From the late nineteenth century it had an Officer Training Corps, a body that went into overdrive during the First World War, as seen here, with pupils being given weapons training behind Percy Currey's 1894 chapel. The school produced a considerable number of officers in the period. Many were commissioned into the Sherwood Foresters (Notts. & Derbys.) and the Derbyshire Imperial Yeomanry, and they sustained sufficient casualties to fill three large plaques on the war memorial erected in front of the building in 1920, to designs by Sir Reginald Blomfield.

1917 Sir Thomas 'Tommy Ditto' Roe (1832–1923) was twice MP for Derby (1883–95) and (1900–17) and three times mayor, the last time in 1910. He was a Liberal councillor and alderman from 1859 until 1914, and was raised to the peerage in 1917 as 1st Lord Roe of Derby, the first Derby-born peer to have still been a resident of the borough at his elevation. He acquired his nickname during his parliamentary career from his habit, on hearing a speech with which he concurred, of leaping to his feet and bellowing 'And I say ditto to that, Mr Speaker!' He married the daughter of the Midland Railway's locomotive superintendent, Matthew Kirtley, but died without issue in 1923.

PARKFIELDS CEDARS,
The future home of the
Derby Municipal Secondary School
for Girls.

1917 By the beginning of the century, the Higher Grade Board School, later the Derby Municipal Secondary School for Girls, in Abbey Street was regarded as inadequate. Further, there was no girls' equivalent to Derby School, so the municipality decided to create a girls' grammar school, and bought the house and 5-acre estate of Parkfield(s) Cedars, Kedleston Road. The school reopened there in April 1917 and flourished until 6 February 1965 when the building burned down. Exactly four years later the school itself became a comprehensive and moved to the edge of the vast new municipal estate at nearby Mackworth, and the (replacement) buildings were taken over as the County Council's Schools' Resources Centre.

1919 The High Sheriff arrives at the Shire Hall in St Mary's Gate for the opening of the Assizes, which were held here from its building in 1660 until 1971, when it became a Crown court. Here the High Sheriff for 1919–20, Albert Leslie Wright of Butterley Hall – a director of the famous Butterley Company – arrives in his carriage with his pikemen and trumpeters. On the right is the corner of the Judges' Lodgings of 1810–12. The whole complex, cruelly abandoned by the County Council after the opening of a new Crown court in The Morledge in 1989, was, following a long battle to save significant portions, converted into magistrates' courts, 2001–4.

1919 The view along Queen Street from the top of Iron Gate by the west door of the Cathedral towards St Michael's Church. All the left-hand range was due to be demolished for street widening. The iron railings of 1873 in front of the Cathedral (which replaced the set from the incomparable hand of Robert Bakewell, lost during a previous widening scheme) were removed in 1942. Beyond them can be seen the early seventeenth-century Bull's Head Inn, founded by Derby's first mayor, Henry Mellor (who died in office in 1637: an inauspicious start!). It was pulled down to widen the top of Full Street in 1942 and its vernacular wrought-iron sign is now in Derby Museum.

1919 This is the counterpart view to the photograph on p. 31, taken by Hurst & Wallis, also for the borough surveyor, eight years later. It shows Osmaston Road, looking back towards The Spot, with an interesting range of late eighteenth- and early nineteenth-century buildings, mainly replaced in the 1930s. Palin's motorcycle showroom, right, is especially evocative, displaying the names of Ariel, Matchless, New Hudson, Norton, AJS, HRD and Omega.

The 1920s

1920   Sadler Gate Bridge is a short section of street connecting the lower end of Sadler Gate with Bold Lane and Cheapside, created on the north side of the Markeaton Brook from the late seventeenth century. The bridge itself disappeared in 1870 when the brook was culverted and The Strand created. In this photograph, taken from where Derby Museum shop now stands, the scene includes, from left to right, a Victorian shop, a late eighteenth-century one, a particularly fine early eighteenth-century shop-fronted house and a late Regency shop – all demolished in favour of a motor garage a couple of decades later. The garage itself was later modified into a shop and is now closed and awaiting redevelopment.

1920 Before the final implementation of the Central Improvement Plan (see introduction), Full Street followed the line of the Derwent before sweeping into a constricted near-alley beside the 1764 Assembly Rooms and debouching into the Market Place. This view, taken by Assistant Borough Surveyor C.B. Sherwin, shows the point where this transition was made. The Horse & Trumpet Inn (ever known to locals as the 'Whore & Strumpet') was built around 1714, although certain record of it does not occur until 1761. Horace Ramsden was its landlord during most of the 1920s, but it was acquired by Offiler's, the Derby brewery company, and demolished in 1939, being replaced in a style best described as 'stockbroker clerk's Tudor'. The building to the left is the County Assembly of 1714 (Derby's first Assembly Rooms), which became redundant and was converted into a showroom in 1764. All was cleared away in 1967 to make way for the present Assembly Rooms (1977) and its multi-storey car park.

1921 From the 1890s terraces of what estate agents call 'palisaded villas' grew up in New Normanton, one complex of such streets being named after the military heroes of the South African War. In this picture, taken on 9 June, we see 23 Powell Street (named after Baden-Powell, of course, but rarely pronounced correctly!) with Mr Alfred John Offen – a solicitor and junior partner with Messrs Moody & Woolley – apparently leaving for work (on his wife's bicycle!) while Mrs Offen looks on. The plaque on the door reads 'A.J. Offen, Solicitor'. He later became a senior partner and moved to a new detached house nearby in Horwood Avenue in 1930. Neither house has changed much in the intervening period, bar the loss of the cast-iron railings in 1942.

1921 With the end of the First World War, a rash of war memorials was set up all over Derby: public, private, corporate and church ones. Over 130 have been recorded. Many were in Ashford Black Marble and Chellaston alabaster – two local ornamental stones – and the work extended the life of spar manufacturers R.G Lomas & Co. for a decade. This rather modest memorial was that of the Rose Hill Wesleyan Chapel, put up on the wall of the mission room in the autumn of 1921, and here being unveiled by a local notable.

1922 The popularisation of motor travel led to the motor charabanc which, being much more flexible than trains or horse-drawn wagons, made group outings popular. Postcards of pub outings are particularly common in Derby, although this rare one depicts twenty-eight men from the long-defunct Curzon Arms, on the corner of Abbey Street and Monk Street, about to set off for Skegness in a solid-tyred vehicle. The inn, probably founded when the two streets were pitched around 1825, had not long to run: it was closed and demolished in 1929; the site (typically) has been a car park ever since.

41

1922 Modern scholars consider that there were at least eight pre-conquest parish churches in Derby, although only six are mentioned in Domesday Book. Two became the focus of twelfth-century monastic foundations. St Mary's, at the top (east) end of St Mary's Gate, vanished in the early fifteenth century, but the rest were flourishing in 1900. Today, two have become redundant: St Werburgh's is still looking for a viable use but the other has been demolished. The clearing of the buildings opposite All Saints' in 1921 for street widening revealed the footings of St Mary's, which C.B. Sherwin excavated in advance of new building in 1922; previously even the site of this church had been a mystery.

1923 In 1861 the new cattle market was opened beside the Derwent, and a wholesale market grew up adjacent; this was finally replaced in 1967, when the inner ring-road invaded the site. This evening view shows packing up at the end of a market day there, with a fascinating collection of vehicles – some, even then, almost museum pieces – on parade.

1924 In the 1920s boundary changes and improvements to public transport and the motor car saw much suburban development, and this in turn started to take its toll on the larger houses and their extensive grounds. The first casualty was Derwent Bank, shown here, the magnificent villa built as Darley Grove for five-times-married silk throwster Thomas Bridgett in 1825. After the death in 1922 of the widow of its last owner, the house was demolished. Mercifully, part of its park was added in 1931 to the adjacent Darley Park. For most of the nineteenth century it had been the property of Edward Strutt, 1st Lord Belper, whose executors sold off some of the grounds for housing in 1877 – hence the area known as 'Strutt's Park'.

1924 A view of The Morledge from the roof of Sir Alfred Haslam's huge Ice Factory, looking towards the Shot Tower. Cockpit Hill market is on the extreme left. The stalls here were all banished to the open market, covering part of the paint works on the middle right a decade later, and the area around the iron *pissoir* became the bus station. Somehow, the Cockpit Hill area and market survived until 1970. The skyline is marked by (left to right) the dome of the Derby Co-operative Society's Central Suite; the Corn Exchange and the Guildhall. To the right of the Shot Tower is the tower of All Saints'.

1924 One of Derby's streets containing the most contrast was Babington Lane, pitched in 1789 to improve the way to Burton. It once boasted Babington House, a mansion of 1626, Abbott's Hill House of 1715, the Grand Theatre and this extraordinary row of cottages built into a malting house of early nineteenth-century date. The man responsible was Chellaston-born entrepreneur Alderman Robert Foreman, Mayor of Derby in 1848–9. The malting floor occupied the first-floor level, and the rooms of the cottages were on the south side, with their street doors on the north, fronting the upper reaches of Babington Lane – hence the windowless façade seen in this photograph taken by Sherwin on 25 November 1925. They were demolished in 1927–8, and the site is now a car park, tyre centre and tannery.

1925 Sam Adams was a tripe dresser. He is shown here posing at his shop door at 27 Albert Street; it is a moot point what today's health inspectorate, let alone EC regulations, would make of his display today. Indeed, one wonders what they'd make of a tripe shop at all! The shop with its good, if plain, early nineteenth-century shop-front and, indeed, the premises, are long gone.

1925 On 21 February the Mechanics' Institute celebrated its centenary; it was founded by the sons of Jedediah Strutt and other Whiggish luminaries of the Derby Philosophical Society 'to improve the educational lot of the artisan classes'. The magnificent Greek Revival building in The Wardwick was built to designs of William Mansfield Cooper in 1836. Although rebuilt in 1882, the magnificence of the lecture hall is still apparent in this photograph of the centenary dinner, presided over by the Duke of Devonshire. After the Second World War the hall was divided up as a shopping arcade, but was restored to something close to its original appearance and opened as a drinking establishment in May 2000.

1925 Derby Market Place, complete with stalls, photographed on a wet 22 May 1925. The west (far) side of the Market Place is largely unchanged – only the third building from the left, Austin's, a former town house of about 1697, has gone. It was replaced by Martin's Bank a decade after this view was taken. The scaffolding (right) marks the erection of Messrs Barlow & Taylor's new store (now the Derbyshire Building Society), their former premises being immediately to the right of the central lamp standard. The prominent central building is Smith's Bank, designed by Thomas Isborne, 1878, now the Natwest. The stalls were all tidied away to the new open market in 1934, leaving the Market Place somewhat soul-less, especially today with the 1977 Assembly Rooms complex towering over its north side.

1925 James Harwood was born at Colchester in 1841, and came to Derby in 1863 to work for Bemrose & Co. In 1870 he opened a stationer's shop in Cornmarket, and by the time of his death in January 1925 he had built it up to be the biggest stationery and printing business in the town. In 1879 he had founded and published the famous *ABC Railway Guides*, which made his fortune. He also built up one of the finest collections of antiques and fine art in the borough, which he crammed into his fine house at 73 Wilson Street (on the corner of Green Lane), designed and built in 1851 by T.C. Hine of Nottingham. This photograph of the sitting room was taken for the catalogue for the sale of his collections by Messrs Richardson & Linnell on 23–24 June 1925. The business finally closed in 1999.

1926 Another casualty of Derby's expanding suburbs was Chaddesden Hall, purchased by a development company and demolished in this year. It had been built by the Wilmots in 1727 on the site of its predecessor, erected in 1639. As the Wilmots – Derby drapers grown rich on the spoils of the Dissolution of the Monasteries – were 'of Chaddesden' from at least 1539, it must be assumed that this was their third house. Chaddesden Lane runs in front. The park and some of the estate was leased to Chaddesden parish council, who transferred it to Derby County Borough for ninety-nine years at £250 per annum. Later they acquired the freehold, totalling 60 acres, for £11,000; they preserved the core of the parkland and built municipal housing over the remainder.

1926 Derby Assembly Rooms. The building was designed by local amateur architect and retired admiral Washington Shirley, 5th Earl Ferrers, and built in 1763–4 by Joseph Pickford of Derby, with the interiors by Robert Adam a decade later. The building to the right was contemporary, to house the catering for the Assemblies, while to the left can be seen the narrow neck of Full Street. The house in the distance, no. 3, was inhabited by Dr Erasmus Darwin FRS from 1783 to 1802, and was demolished in 1933. On the left is Messrs Pountain's, vintners, whose 1876 building by James Wright was demolished in 1970. The façade of the Assembly Rooms was re-erected at Crich Tramway Museum in 1971; the remainder had already been demolished after a minor fire in 1963.

1926 A new fish market was built at the south end of the 1864 Market Hall and opened in 1926; this photograph was one of a set taken to mark the event. At least one of the firms which operated there at the opening, Roome's, is still flourishing, three generations on, with a shop in Sadler Gate.

1927 Until 1884 Derbyshire had been part of the grea
Mercian Diocese of Lichfield, but in that year it was
combined with Nottingham to form the Diocese of
Southwell. In 1927 the county became a separate dioces
St Werburgh's was originally intended to become the
Cathedral, but the former Corporation Church of All
Saints' was ultimately chosen. The first Bishop was the R
Revd Dr Edmund Courtenay Pearce (1870–1935)
formerly Master of Corpus Christi, Cambridge. He was
also an ex-Mayor of Cambridge and ex-Chairman of
Cambridgeshire County Council, an unexpected
combination of talents which probably stood him in good
stead in Derbyshire!

1927 Derby Children's Hospital was founded in the 1870s and in 1883 moved into handsome, purpose-built premises i
North Street, Strutt's Park; it was one of the earliest designs of Alexander MacPherson (1847–1935). It closed in 1996 an
was demolished two years later, the site being developed for 'executive homes'. This photograph of the matron, six sisters an
fifteen nurses was taken in the hospital's heyday in 1927, a decade before the complex was extended in 'pavilion' style b
T.H. Thorpe.

1921 One of the few gentry town houses to retain its garden at this period was 35 St Mary's Gate, built in 1730 for the Batemans of Hartington Hall and sold to Blyth Simpson, attorney, whose family twice enlarged it, running their legal practice therefrom and living 'over the shop'. It was still the home of Sancroft Grimwood Taylor, the senior partner of Messrs Taylor, Simpson & Mosley, the practice founded by Blyth Simpson. The firm moved out 2005 and the grade II* listed building is currently in the hands of a developer.

1928 Municipal housing, after a slow start locally, proceeded apace from the mid-1920s, and the more so after the boundary extension of 1928. In this year new artificial stone block housing is seen under construction in Sinfin, well to the south of the fledgling ring-road (or Derby Arterial Road as it was known at the time).

1928 In 1922 Derby Borough Council decided to use part of Osmaston Park to build the 'New British Speedway' circuit with a lap distance of one-third of a mile. The project was also intended to provide work for unemployed labourers. Professor A.M. Low was recruited to compute the correct banking angles to accommodate speeds of 80 mph. Needless to say, the project looked like being a white elephant, for it was from the outset too small for motor-cycling. However, it was successfully adapted for bicycle championships, and served well in that role until after 1945, although the banking was considered too steep for cycling. Percy, Ralph and Fred Wyld were three brothers who rose to the pinnacle of achievement in the late 1920s as international cycling champions. Fred – seen here about to start a race in 1928 – won five titles in this year alone.

1928   The tramways lasted until 1932, when they were replaced by trolleybuses over a two-year period. This view, taken outside the Spotted Horse Inn in Victoria Street, shows Brush (Loughborough)-built car no. 68 (of 1926) about to depart for Uttoxeter Road (Constable Lane) on route 12, which originated in Burton Road. The Derby tramways were laid to the unusual gauge of 4 ft and lengths of track still appear during city centre roadworks.

1929   The Old Bell Hotel, Sadler Gate, is a fine four-gabled three-storey brick inn built around 1680 as a coaching inn. Today, it is the last surviving one in the city. In the 1770s it was bought by the Campion family who ran it for just over a century, adding a fine ballroom at the rear, although Lord Torrington wrote rather scathingly of it when he visited in 1794! The last coach departed in 1855, and in 1928 the inn was taken over by the St James's Hotel company and rebuilt, contractors Messrs Ford & Weston covering the exterior in faux timber-framing using authentic timbers salvaged from demolished country houses. The carriage arch, seen here, was narrowed and lowered, and the ground level raised, so that one can hardly envisage a coach and four turning in!

1929 The Tudor Room at the Old Bell, a 'Gentlemen Only' bar of entirely new build, albeit using architectural salvage and filled with 'period' items including a fine tavern clock (removed in the 1980s) and Lord Bessborough's armour (stolen). The inn, which reopened in 1929, was nearly lost to a plan to convert it to shop units in 1989, but was saved on conservation grounds – it has the finest late seventeenth-century timber staircase in the city – and converted into a 'fun pub'. The Tudor Room was stripped and is now a store.

1929 The Bemrose family came to Derby from Lincolnshire and set up a printing business in 1826. For a century the business expanded, becoming by the 1960s one of the nation's most important printing firms, and the family supplied a succession of cultivated and competent aldermen and mayors. Henry Howe Bemrose FGS (1857–1939) was Chairman of the firm as well as Mayor of Derby in 1909–10. He was also a notable geologist and a great philanthropist, donating a large sum of money to the borough for the establishment of a much-needed second boys' grammar school. This was built on the Uttoxeter Road to the designs of the ubiquitous Alexander MacPherson (his last before retirement) and opened in 1929, duly being named Bemrose School. Its appearance has since been marred by unsympathetic extensions.

1929 A view inside the Market Hall, designed by Borough Surveyor Thomas Thorburn in 1864 and built using iron from the nearby foundry of J. & G. Haywood to form a spectacular vaulted roof. The original stalls remained until the 1930s, and were replaced again in a major refurbishment in 1989. Here, staff of John & Mary Morley's newsagents pose by the stall. Note that *Good Housekeeping* included an article by the redoubtable Godfrey Winn, then two years into his successful career as a journalist after giving up acting. To the left is the stall of Frank Woore, one of the most important antiquarian book dealers in the region in his time. He took over from Frank Murray in 1915 and continued until 1959.

The 1930s

1930 Peartree station on the Derby (Midland)–Birmingham line, looking south-east. From 1928 the Derby ring-road was under construction, the expansion of the borough's boundaries in that year making the space available. This section was the last to be completed, although it was only a short stretch, from Newdigate Street to Osmaston Park Road. The municipal houses bounding it can be dimly seen in the distance. The photographer is standing at the entrance to Portland Street (left). The railway runs in a cutting here so little can be seen of the station itself. The widened road was finally opened a year or two later, and the Co-operative Society's impressive Art Deco bakery built beyond. Today there is a large roundabout beyond the bridge giving access to a Sainsbury's Superstore, on the site of the bakery.

1931 Aiton & Co.'s works in Stores Road was completed in this year to an innovative Art Deco design by two women architects, Betty Scott and local girl Norah Aiton (1904–89). The latter was a daughter of Sir John Aiton (1864–1950) who founded the firm (making pipework and allied special equipment) in 1900. The design was at the forefront of Modern architecture, and is the first notable work in that style by women architects, and Derby Civic Society was pleased to be able to get it added to the Statutory List in 1999, by which date it had passed out of the hands of the original firm and was under threat.

1931 The staircase at Aiton's.

1925 Babington Lane, on the corner of Gower Street. In this photograph, taken from beneath the canopy of the Grand Theatre, can be seen the garden wall of Abbott's Hill House (visible to the left). The house was built in 1715 by Simon Degge FRS, and was later the home of Alderman Foreman, who built the eccentric maltings-cum-cottages nearby (see p. 44). It was demolished in 1926. The garden wall appears to have been considerably raised when the street was pitched in 1789.

1979 Hunter's furnishing store, built in 1931 on the same site as that shown above, to designs by Naylor & Sale of Derby, and still flourishing.

1932 On the night of Saturday/Sunday 21/22 May 1932 the last of Derby's great floods occurred; it was the worst since 1 April 1842. Water backing up the Derwent from the Trent, itself in flood, blocked the flow of flood water from the Peak down the Derwent, and caused the Markeaton Brook, long culverted, to overflow to the height of several feet, as shown here in Cornmarket. To make matters worse, a gas blast wrecked H. Samuel's shop on the Monday morning after this view was taken.

(Inset) Efforts to rescue flooded stock and take preventative measures were hampered by crowds of glum sightseers, but at least some of the local children enjoyed themselves! They are pictured outside Woolworth's in Victoria Street having a wonderful time, although the boy on the right was clearly obliged by his mother to go out smartly dressed in his school uniform. In the 1840s Herbert Spencer had proposed building a movable barrier across the Derwent at Alvaston to prevent floods of this type but, then a young man, he was ignored by the corporation. Interestingly, it was built within nine months of the 1932 disaster in which, amazingly, only one life was lost.

1932 A new gaol was built in 1826 to the designs of Francis Goodwin, who set it in a carefully planned enclave to the south of Friar Gate. It was decommissioned in 1926, and most of the buildings were demolished in 1928. In this view, work is under way to turn the site into a greyhound stadium. Note the original entrance block in the distance. This was massively constructed in stone in Doric style and was flanked by bastions added after the 'reform riot' of October 1832. These bastions, and the massive flanking walls, were allowed to remain. The track was closed in 1988 and a mixed residential/office development in a weak Neo-Georgian style was built on the site, again retaining most of Goodwin's façade.

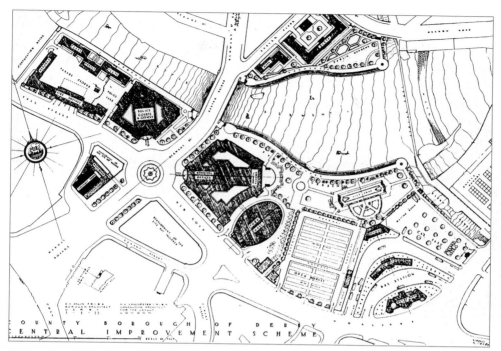

1933 The published plan of the Central Improvement Scheme of that year, designed by C.H. Aslin CBE (1893–1959), the newly appointed borough architect. It envisaged clearing a whole swathe of works – including the Shot Tower – between The Morledge, Tenant Street and the river, and the building of council offices, an oval council chamber, an open market, a parabolic bus station (shaped to match the constrictions of the site), a car park and the River Gardens. Morledge was to be extended on a new alignment to meet Full Street, to be renamed Corporation Street, and to the north-west of the bridge (renewed in 1929) were to be magistrates' courts, the police station and a fire station, grouped round a parade ground. The 1764 Assembly Rooms are shown as extended. Only the intervention of the war prevented completion along the lines set out.

1933 The Central Improvement Scheme was implemented with considerable speed, the open market (which gave the corporation an excuse to remove the market stalls from both the Market Place and the Morledge) being inaugurated in 1933. Aslin's strengths were a fine sense of proportion, attention to detail and a nice line in ornamental metalwork. Here these virtues are apparent in the boundary fencing: wrought iron, very simple but of exceptional proportions and with satisfying touches of detail.

1933   On 22 April Sir (Frederick) Henry Royce OBE, 1st (and last) Bt, co-founder of Rolls-Royce and engineering genius, died. He brought his new company to Derby in 1907, and resided at The Knoll, Quarndon, but retired to West Wittering in Sussex after suffering a total breakdown in health in 1911. His diversification into the manufacture of aero engines turned an important motor manufacturer into a vast organisation of international renown, carried on in his absence and after his death by a few well-chosen lieutenants and a skilled and loyal workforce. Few people have had a statue erected in their honour in their own lifetime, but Derby's sculpture by Francis Derwent Wood RA was unveiled in the arboretum in 1923. Like most Derby statues, it has moved twice since. After the war it went to the River Gardens (where it is seen here in 1978) and in 1988 was moved to Rolls-Royce HQ on Sinfin Moor.

1933   On 3 May, a dismal day, HRH the Duke of York, later King George VI, visited Derby to make a series of morale-boosting visits to local firms, then feeling the full effects of the Great Depression. After going to Rolls-Royce, he is seen here arriving at Ley's foundry in Peartree. Founded in 1874, Ley's Malleable Castings company soon acquired a licence to produce the US Ewart chain belt, and swiftly became a firm of national importance, earning a baronetcy for its baseball-promoting founder, Sir Francis Ley. The firm flourished until it was taken over by a 1980s Derby success story, Williams Holdings PLC, which closed the works on 2 April 1987 and sold the site for redevelopment.

1933 The Derby Central Omnibus Station – to give it its full title – was opened on 8 October 1933, approximately the date of this photograph, taken from the roof of the White Horse inn. Contemporary publicity said of this building that it was 'Quite a new departure with amenities even better than those usually associated with the largest Railway Station and the architecture is wisely in keeping with the scheme.' In fact it was a pioneering design, but in 2005 was demolished for redevelopment, not helped by its failure (through subsequent alterations) to secure addition to the Statutory List. Behind can be seen the 1861 cattle market (closed and demolished for the inner ring-road in 1970).

1934 Derby's slum properties were still being cleared rather slowly at this time, and this view is of Albion Court, looking towards Albion Street. The late eighteenth-century dwellings are in a poor state, and were eventually cleared in 1939. The street beyond had to wait until the 1950s, when it became a shopping street terminating, from 1972, in the notorious Eagle Centre shopping complex. That development was rebuilt in 1993 and completely replaced by Westfield Shoppingtowns in 2006–7.

1934 Another 'problem' property demolished to make way for housing was Darley House. Built in 1790 for the Evans family, who established the Boar's Head cotton mill in Darley Abbey in 1782, Darley House's last manifestation was as a prep school. When the Evans estate was broken up in 1931, it was sold to the corporation which, in a burst of egalitarianism, drove out the school and razed the house. It had been designed by another talented amateur, William Strutt FRS (1756–1831), brother-in-law of Thomas Evans, its owner. Coleridge spent five weeks here in 1796 – 'the happiest of my life' – and stayed again a year later. The Regency mill village which grew up around the house is one of the finest in the UK.

1935 The Great Depression took its toll on the King Street China Factory, seen here a year or two before, and it was taken over by Royal Crown Derby, thus uniting two strands of the history of china manufacture into one firm. This little factory was set up in 1848 on the closure of the original 1750 china factory on Nottingham Road by a group of five of its former employees. In 1859 one of them, Sampson Hancock – a man with two or three generations in the trade behind him – took over the firm, and it was run by his family until closure.

1935 A rare view of the interior of the King Street works.

1935 On 5 June Sir Alan Cobham's 'Flying Circus' came to Derby for a National Aviation Day display. His motley collection of aircraft made their HQ on Stenson Fields, and for 'five bob' one could enjoy (if that is the word) a short flight in an Airspeed AS4 Ferry. These events presaged the coming of Derby Airport, opened just three years later nearby at Burnaston (see p. 64).

National Aviation Day Display

Organized by
SIR ALAN COBHAM, K.B.E., A.F.C.

VALID FOR ONE FLIGHT

5/-

PER PASSENGER

SUBJECT TO CONDITIONS OVERLEAF

Issued by National Aviation Displays Ltd.,
Grand Buildings, Trafalgar Square, London, W.C. 2

To be Retained by Passenger

1936 Frank Gresley, a notable Chellaston resident died aged eighty in 1936. The second in a dynasty of four talented artists, Frank was the son of James Stephen Gresley (1829–1908), one of a family of Sandiacre lace manufacturers, who was the first artist in the family, specialising in landscapes, mainly in oils. Frank painted Trent Valley landscapes in both oil and watercolours, and his works are much sought after today. He married into a notable dynasty of Derby pub landlords and two of his sons, Cuthbert (1876–1963) and Harold (1892–1969) also became artists. Cuthbert worked primarily for Royal Crown Derby, while Harold was probably the most accomplished of the entire family. This is his portrait of his father in his later years.

1936 Although the arboretum already had a bandstand, Herbert Aslin designed a new one in Art Deco style which was inaugurated in 1936. Here we see a concert in full swing on a Sunday afternoon. The building, like the park itself, suffered from neglect and vandalism after the war, being burnt out by arsonists in 1997.

1937 The age of the cinema was still dominant in 1937 when a new one was built to serve Normanton at the Cavendish a road intersection and shopping centre which took its name from a pub at the southern extremity of New Normanton, just inside the ring road. Just three more cinemas were to be built – all in the suburbs – before war broke out two years later. The Cavendish was built at a cost of £30,000 on the site of the Derby Pavilion, an 'end-of-the-pier' type variety venue which burnt down in 1929 after a 24-year existence. It was opened by Mayor E.E. Paulson on 28 December 1937 with a showing of 'For You Alone'. J. Arthur Rank bought it in 1942 and it was closed on 19 December 1960, the site being turned into a Fine Fare (now Somerfield) supermarket.

1938 A view up St Peter's Street from Babington Lane to The Spot. Queen Victoria was by now long gone (see p. 31), and the corner building behind had just been replaced by the most adventurous design of its date in Derby – by Sir Frederick Bennett & Partners of London for a development company, whose tenant was Messrs Eastern's. Behind looms the bulk of the Gaumont Palace cinema of 1934, one of the few surviving such buildings in Derby and architecturally the most distinguished. This area is now pedestrianised and has a new 'feature' built on the Spot island over the public loos in weak municipal Art Deco Revival style; incorporating a clock tower (with clock by John Smith of Derby); it is known locally as the 'gun emplacement'.

1938 This year saw the loss of the greater part of one of Derby's most distinguished domestic buildings, St Mary's Gate House, seen here boarded up. It was built in 1731 for the Osborne family and was decorated with much beautiful wrought ironwork by Robert Bakewell. It passed by inheritance to the Bateman family in 1777, and they later sold it to Samuel Evans of Darley Hall. In 1842 it was converted into Derby's Baptist Chapel by James Fenton of Chelmsford. When this closed, it was purchased by Sir George Kenning, the Chesterfield-born garage proprietor, who had premises behind. His firm razed the building to provide car storage space, and part of the St Mary's Gate front was sold to an insurance company to build offices. The main gate and one side gate are now at Derby Cathedral; the urns from the roof and the rest of the ironwork went to Barton Blount Hall.

1938 Osmaston Hall, perhaps the largest of the country houses within the city, was built by the Wilmots in 1697 to designs by Sir William Wilson. As the Wilmot-Hortons, they let it to the Fox family in the 1840s, and in 1888 it was sold to the Midland Railway, who sold the estate where it bounded London Road to build the suburb-let of Wilmorton (see p. 24). They laid a siding almost to the front door, and used the Hall for offices and storage. The LMS sold it to Derby Corporation, which demolished it in 1938; work is seen here well under way.

1938 The interior, seen here in a photograph taken in the 1870s, was a very fine one. The site of the house was developed after the war as an industrial estate, this process also putting paid to the tiny church of St James, Osmaston, as well as the graveyard, vicarage and lodges.

1938 Burnaston House, a Soanian-style neo-Greek villa, was saved from destruction when its park was bought to build Derby Airport, opened in August 1938. The house became the terminal building and club house. In this view a group of senior police and fire officials have just disembarked from the De Havilland DH89A Dragon Rapide after assessing its potential in their work. The aircraft was owned by Derby Aviation Ltd, later Derby Airways and now British Midland. Commercial flying was transferred to Castle Donington after the war, but Burnaston was reopened for private flying in 1987. Four years later the site was given to Toyota to build a hideously intrusive motor-car factory, and the house, previously saved from demolition, was in the process of a grant-aided restoration when compulsorily purchased and destroyed.

1939 Derby has only one building by the great Sir Edwin Lutyens – the Midland Railway war memorial cenotaph in Midland Road – but a striking branch of Marks & Spencer in St Peter's Street, designed by his son Robert (then the firm's architect), was completed in 1937 in a semi-Classical style with Art Deco detailing. In 1939 it was joined by a branch of Montague Burton's, sheathed in black marble. This supplemented a much bigger branch nearby in Victoria Street built almost a decade earlier. This branch, however, has now vanished.

65

1939 Hospital Day was always an excuse for a great deal of fun, with a procession featuring a large number of decorated floats going from the Derbyshire Royal Infirmary – then run by an independent trust for which the event was an important fund-raiser – to the Market Place. Many other events also took place. This is bandleader Sid Hawker's float, adapted from a Trent bus chassis, about to set out; it was photographed for a postcard (to be sold to raise more funds) by W.W. Winter.

1939 Ford Street, looking east. Behind the lorry can be seen the iron bridge of the former GNR line (by this date the L&NER), which ran on brick arches to Friar Gate station. The huge mill behind was one of several served by the line and built in the 1880s; unlike the line, it still survives, converted into offices. The chapel-like building on the left was the St Werburgh's Mission Room, and on the other side of this medieval thoroughfare (named after a ford through the Markeaton Brook which, by this date, ran under the road) stands the Derby Gas Works of 1820, cleared in the 1960s. Ford Street is now one end of the part-built Derby inner ring road.

1939 One of the memorable events of the 1930s was the sudden disappearance of a steam roller in The Strand in August. Those who built the culvert containing the Markeaton Brook, over which the street was pitched in 1877, probably never anticipated vehicles of such weight being used, and the inevitable happened while the vehicle was en route to its depot after resurfacing work. The thickness of the road surface at the apex of the culvert can be seen in all its thin-ness! The war prevented the full rebuilding of the culvert until the 1960s.

1939 Late summer, and an evening's (illegal) fishing in the Derwent weir, with war just days away. Corporation by-laws forbade fishing here, but nobody seemed to enforce it in those days. In the background is the canal bridge carrying Derwent Row, demolished in the 1960s, when the weir, too, was rebuilt – it is now higher and steeper.

War and Austerity

1940 Evidence of air raid precautions is apparent in this view of Andrew
Handyside & Co.'s 1876 Friar Gate Bridge, looking along Friar Gate from
the town centre towards Ashbourne Road. The trolleybus poles are banded
with white stripes, the Morris 8 has its headlights obscured and no doubt
the light bulbs have been removed from the railway carrriages of the LNER
train passing over the bridge into Derby (Friargate) station. In the distance
the Corporation Omnibus Department's tower wagon is parked by the
former home of Joseph Pickford, the eighteenth-century architect (since
1988 a museum) while the linesmen have a sandwich lunch. With
restrictions on car use, little traffic is in evidence on this May day.

1941 The night of 15/16 January 1941 saw one of Derby's two serious air raids. Forty-nine enemy aircraft attacked in three waves between 8 pm and 4 am, dropping 59 tons of high explosives and nearly 1,500 incendiary bombs, badly damaging the Midland station, Bliss's factory in Little Chester and houses in Offerton Avenue, Derby Lane, Rose Hill Street, Litchurch Street and Canal Street, killing 20 people and injuring 48. Fortunately, the raid was hampered by low cloud. This photograph shows the effect of the bomb that wrecked the old arboretum bandstand, debris from which destroyed Coffee's florentine boar (see p. 25).

1945 The outbreak of war stalled the Central Improvement Scheme, with the planned council chamber unbuilt and the council offices unfinished. The latter were rapidly made habitable – certain aspects of the building were never finished as intended – and requisitioned, and the building was formally opened by Princess Elizabeth on 27 June 1947. This picture taken in the summer of 1945, shows Aslin's inspired handling of the south-east angle, overlooking the River Gardens, in Neo-Wren style, with the 'Boy and Goose' statue given to the town in 1928 by the widow of Lord Roe (see p. 36) in front. This statue was designed by Charles Clayton Thompson of Derby, made by R.G. Lomas & Co. of King Street, and cast by Alexander Fisher of Chelsea, and had previously stood by the old Assembly Rooms in the Market Place. It is now the centrepiece of a memorial garden to the late Sir Peter Hilton nearby.

1946 The opposite side of the Council House also boasted a round point: a traffic island – much less attractive. After the war the planned council chamber never materialised, and instead Aslin's successor built one within the inner courtyard of the council offices. In the distance, nothing has changed in sixty-one years, but on the right there was to be a most serious casualty: the Old Mayor's Parlour in Tenant Street, built in 1487. The largest timber-framed town house of its date in the UK, it was once the home of England's pioneering proto-gynaecologist, Dr Percival Willoughby (1596–1685). Sadly, it seems that it was visible from the mayor's offices opposite and in 1948 it was demolished, although no use was ever found for the site. An offer from the Derbyshire Archaeological Society to purchase the building was ignored and it missed being listed by months.

1947 Derby Market Head, with the corner of Iron Gate (right) and Sadler Gate (left) with Lloyd's Bank in between. This fine building dates from the later 1690s and was the house of the Drewry family, publishers of the *Derby Mercury* from the early eighteenth century until 1826, when William Bemrose bought it. At the turn of the century his successors sold it to the bank, who rebuilt the ground floor in Victorian style. In 1953, however, they cruelly gutted the interior and replaced the roof with a flat one, rather spoiling its appearance. The building beside it to the right is the former George inn of 1693, by this date the Globe tavern, later the Mr Jorrocks, the George (again), from 1997 to 2003 Lafferty's Irish Bar and since then has reverted to Mister Jorrocks.

71

1947 The Derby Canal was barely used before the war began, and afterwards it was totally moribund, as shown in this picture of the stretch beside Siddall's Road towards the basin by Cockpit Hill. The mill, left, was built as a cheese warehouse in 1842–3 by no less than Francis Thompson, architect of the station; its hoist apertures seem recently (and ineptly) blocked up. The big mill beyond was once Oliver Wilkins & Co.'s colour works, by 1935 taken over by ICI. In the 1970s, shortly before being demolished to build a new road to the railway station over the line of the canal (abandoned in 1964), it was making yellow tar paint for road markings.

1947 One of Derby's most attractive buildings had been designed for the School Board in 1880 and built in Becket Street by William Giles. When the Boards were abolished in 1903, the council took over as the education authority, working from the same building. However, the reorganisation consequent on the opening of the Council House meant that the old building became redundant. Thus, in advance of its new role, the council took the trouble to get two of its workforce to chip the 'Derby School Board' legend off the parapet.

1948 A view down St Peter's Street from opposite St Peter's churchyard (south side). The chancel of St Peter's is on the left, and on the right the exciting white terracotta façade of the Whitehall Picture Theatre by T.H. Thorpe of 1914. By this time it was the Odeon and was showing Abbott and Costello in 'The Moose Hangs High'. It closed in 1965 and was demolished to make way for a branch of British Home Stores. Note the magnet symbol still in situ beyond, 'pulling' customers to the Midland Drapery.

1948 Rockhouse Road was one of the very few streets of private housing built before the war in Boulton, where a huge complex of municipal estates went up. The houses were built just before the outbreak of war out of 'Stanley Building Blocks' produced by Tom Anthony of Stanley from the by-products of his quarry in the village of that name. His firm also built the houses, and others are still to be found scattered all over the city. The street was named, of course, after the building material, and Anthony Drive, Anthony Crescent and Stanley Road were all nearby! Shortly after this photograph was taken, the street was adopted and surfaced, and Strathmore Avenue was pitched across in the foreground.

1948 Cornmarket, on a dull Sunday morning, looking north towards the cathedral; the alignment is that of the fossilised line of the prehistoric trackway which passed north–south through the future site of Derby. On the left is part of the Royal Hotel of 1839, by Robert Wallace of London, just four years from closure and conversion into DHSS offices; the former Derby and Derbyshire Bank (labelled Westminster Bank here) next door was designed by the same architect in 1836, and is now a building society. Most of the range beyond was rebuilt in very unsympathetic style in the 1960s. Cornmarket is now pedestrianised and briefly sported a specially designed ornamental iron screen of 1992 across its width near the junction with Victoria Street, in the foreground and was removed in 2004.

1949 Traffic Street ran alongside the northern park wall of a Queen Anne country house called Castlefields – long demolished – and connected London Road with Siddall's Road. It was pitched in the 1830s. In 1937–8, it was widened and realigned debouching onto Cockpit Hill. The surviving artisans' cottages on the old alignment are seen here, not long before they too were cleared. The area was finally developed in the early 1960s as Main Centre – a truly horrible 'shopping precinct', mercifully redeveloped in 2007. The whole of the area between Albion Street and Traffic Street was packed with similar housing; all had gone by 1970.

The 1950s

1950 A foggy morning in Upper Hill Street, a small area of artisans' housing built before 1820. The area was shortly to be cleared – although the process ultimately took almost a decade – and was eventually redeveloped with a group of retail units along Bradshaw Way, formerly Bradshaw Street (widened as part of the inner ring road in 1963). The spire in the background is of the Osmaston Road Baptist Chapel, built by T.C. Hine of Nottingham in 1861–2, and demolished in 1968 in favour of a smaller, more compact, Modernist one.

1952   The Derby Canal, although hardly used after 1939, lingered on. This photograph is of the canal basin, Cockpit Hill. A half-submerged narrow boat appears to have foundered where it was left some twenty years before at the Bridgewater Wharf. The warehouse beside it, a listed building dated 1820, survived the filling in of the canal, which began piecemeal from this period, to form an elegantly decaying centrepiece in a car park built in the middle of a very large traffic island created in 1968, only to be heedlessly swept away a decade later. The site is now occupied by one of the most colossal and hideous multi-storey car parks in the region, completed in 1999.

1952   The canal crossed the Derwent beyond the Cockpit Hill basin, the level of the river being maintained by a weir, and pipes were laid along the canal's course under the Long Bridge, carrying the towpath (see p. 81) at this point, so that the water would not flow into the river and cascade over the weir, leaving the Erewash arm dry. Having crossed the river, the canal went under Derwent Row, seen here, and into White Bear lock, named after the White Bear inn beside it (right). The inn was built about 1820 by Alexander Street, who ran Derby's only canal boat building business from an adjacent yard, and the family ran both until 1877. The whole area – very close to Herbert Spencer's birthplace (see p. 26) – was bulldozed in November 1969.

1953 Ex-Midland Railway and LMS 2P class 4–4–0 locomotive no. 40404 waits its turn outside Derby Midland station. Built at Derby works in April 1892, it survived until June 1957 – a long life for a railway locomotive of this type. In the background can be seen part of the former North Midland Railway locomotive roundhouse of 1839 – the first of its kind in the world. This particular area is now part of Pride Park (see introduction).

1953 References to a well by St Alkmund's Church go back to the twelfth century, although the Derbyshire custom of dressing wells seems only to go back to an early seventeenth-century drought when Tissington was the only village in the White Peak where the water continued to flow. On Whit Tuesday 1870 well-dressings at St Alkmund's well – at the bottom of Well Street, once in St Helen's Park – were inaugurated, and lasted (with the exception of 1940–5), until the church was deconsecrated prior to demolition in 1966. Here the coronation year procession turns from Regency North Parade into early Victorian North Street, well attended and with plenty of sightseers.

1954 Abbey Street, at the bottom of which the Curzon Arms once stood (see p. 41), was pitched, die-straight for nearly half a mile, from Curzon Street to the Burton Road in about 1825. Streets to its west were pitched from 1858, as terraces of housing stretched over what was to become the parish of St Luke – hence Alma Street, seen here, named after the Crimean War battle of 1854. The Housewives' Corner was a typical inexpensive non-grocery 'corner' shop of late Victorian date. This range was demolished in the 1970s in anticipation of the completion of the inner ring road, which has still not materialised.

1955 Rowditch Farm, with Rowditch brickworks beyond, photographed from the ring road (Kingsway), near Thornhill. The 1920s municipal New Zealand estate lies in the distance, left, with the line of the railway in between. The site has been developed subsequently as an 'out of town' shopping complex.

1956 In this year a start was made in clearing a small enclave of extremely poor artisans' cottages called Little City. This had been built immediately after the Napoleonic Wars by Alderman Thomas Madeley, whose Haarlem Mill the inhabitants served. Little City was situated at the top of Green Lane at its junction with Burton Road, and lay virtually opposite Unity Hall (see p. 27). Here the first houses in Cannon Street have been condemned and 'tinned-up' prior to demolition.

1957 Inside the Market Hall, where the stalls have now been replaced (see p. 52). This is C.E. Gibson's hardware stall.

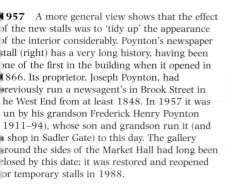

1957 A more general view shows that the effect of the new stalls was to 'tidy up' the appearance of the interior considerably. Poynton's newspaper stall (right) has a very long history, having been one of the first in the building when it opened in 1866. Its proprietor, Joseph Poynton, had previously run a newsagent's in Brook Street in the West End from at least 1848. In 1957 it was run by his grandson Frederick Henry Poynton (1911–94), whose son and grandson run it (and a shop in Sadler Gate) to this day. The gallery around the sides of the Market Hall had long been closed by this date; it was restored and reopened for temporary stalls in 1988.

1958 Cornmarket again, looking north towards the Cathedral. The corner shop (right), Jefferson's, was only the secon
commercial occupant of the premises, the building having been put up in 1848 for Messrs George & George, drapers, wh
moved further up St Peter's Street in the 1860s, and were taken over by Thurman & Malin in 1879, the latter closing ninet
five years later. Robert Jefferson took over the premises in about 1868, and this firm was succeeded on the site after exactly
century by H. Samuel – still there – displaced from Cornmarket by the building of Littlewood's store. The distinct humpe
effect of the roadway in the foreground is caused by the presence of St Peter's Bridge beneath, left in situ when Albert Stree
was formed by culverting in 1848 and revealed by road works in 2004.

1959 The first houses in the old West End, a desperatel
poor area formed by an Act of 1792 enclosing the land
between Friar Gate and Kedleston Road, began to be
condemned in this year. The Markeaton Brook flowed
through the centre of the area, so a large number of
narrow tapes and silk mills grew up along its course in
the very early nineteenth century, interspersed with
housing of generally poor quality. The twentieth-century
inhabitants of the area developed an exceptional *esprit-de-
corps* in their adversity, which was lost when the area wa
redeveloped with municipal flats that were themselves so
poor that they had to be largely rebuilt or replaced in the
1980s and '90s. In this view of Brook Street, Banks's mil
on the corner of Bridge Street (which ran down to elegan
Friar Gate), towers over the pawnshop of Wellington
Pickering, founded in the 1880s and still playing a critica
role in local people's lives after the Second World War. Th
wrought iron sign is now stored in Derby Museum.

1959 The Long Bridge – carrying the Derby canal towpath over the Derwent – lasted from 1796 until 1959. The year before, it had been condemned as dangerous, and on the evidence of this view, that seems not to have been exaggerated! The picture was taken from near Derwent Row Bridge (see p. 76), looking across to the southern edge of the River Gardens. That it survived as long as it did is remarkable.

1951 An atmospheric view looking north up the Derwent from the southern end of the Riverside Gardens towards the silk mill. The power station was built from 1893 right behind the cathedral, but was demolished in 1972, leaving the site green – an inspired move. Right of centre is the silk mill, built for Sir Thomas and John Lombe by the Derby engineer George Sorocold in 1718, rebuilt in 1821, and again in 1910, this time two storeys lower. It opened as Derby Industrial Museum in November 1974. Exeter Bridge, the third on the site, was opened in 1930 as a precursor of the Central Improvement Scheme, having been designed by Charles Arthur Clews, Herbert Aslin's predecessor.

The 1960s

1960 Derby's first 'shopping precinct' was built behind Victoria Street, where ran Becket Well Lane and Summer Hill (see pp. 22, 32), and where stood an interesting and early cinema of 1910, owned and run by three generations of the Duckworth family. This unlovely and doomed development (its last tenants, Harwood's, moved out in 1995) also destroyed the Becket Well, the seventeenth-century stone head of which can be seen in this view of 1960. (Its name was derived from the Norman-French word *bouget*, meaning bucket, and not from St Thomas à Becket, as is often thought.) Work began on the ill-starred scheme in 1960, and although it was listed, the well was taken away and reassembled in the garden of one of the developer's directors at Kirk Langley, where it remains.

1961 Chapel to cinema: this porticoed edifice was built on the corner of London Road and Traffic Street as a Congregational chapel in 1842, being one of the few Classical designs of Derby's best Victorian architect, Henry Isaac Stevens (1806–73). In 1934 it was sold, and converted by Thomas Harrison Thorpe into a cinema named the Coliseum, acquiring a coat of whitewash over its dignified stone façade, a large excrescence on its roof and having the dignity of its Corinthian tetrastyle portico marred by a pair of rooms ineptly added to the extremities. The interior, however, was the finest of Derby's Art-Deco cinema auditoria. It closed on 12 August, the last film being 'Orders are Orders', and was demolished shortly afterwards, to make way for the formation of a traffic island as Phase 1 of the inner ring road, a development that was highly destructive of the townscape.

1963 On St Valentine's night 1963 a fire caused by an electrical fault damaged part of the roof of the 1764 Assembly Rooms (see p. 47), and the council demolished the entire building bar the stone façade. The partly dismantled roof can be seen on the left of this view, taken from the ugly glass tower erected by the county police force the year before in Full Street to extend Aslin's police station. The half-timbered façade is of the old Horse and Trumpet inn as rebuilt (see p. 40), and behind it, lit by four skylights, is the hall of the 1714 County Assembly Rooms, all swept away in 1971 to make way for the new Assembly Rooms and associated car park.

1962 Darley Hall stood on rising ground at the north end of spectacular parkland bordering the Derwent and landscaped by a local follower of Capability Brown, William Emes of Bowbridge Fields (1729–1802). It dominated the pretty Regency mill village of Darley Abbey, created by the Evans family of Darley House (see p. 60). It replaced an earlier hall built from the remains of the dissolved abbey and was built to designs of Francis Smith of Warwick in 1727, being considerably rebuilt by Joseph Pickford of Derby in 1777 for the Holden family, and was latterly listed Grade II*. When the widow of the last Evans died in 1929, it was given, together with 66 acres of park, to the corporation, which installed the old Central School in the building. When the school eventually moved out to new premises in 1961 the hall was preremptorily demolished, although mercifully the stable block and the parkland survive.

1962 Darley Hall: the staircase hall. The guard rail was erected to protect Francis Smith's superb timber staircase from schoolboys. There was also a windvane dial here, put in by John Whitehurst FRS in the 1750s, which survives in Derby Museum.

1964   The destruction did not end there. This is Markeaton Hall, lying in a William Emes park of 211 acres between the Ashbourne and Kedleston Roads, built by Wrightson Mundy in 1755 to designs by James Denstone of Derby. Like Darley Hall, its last proprietor was a widow – Emily Maria Georgiana Mundy, who died in the same year as Mrs Evans – and she bequeathed the house and 16 acres of gardens to the borough for use as an art gallery, or similar. The corporation purchased the park from her heirs but they never found a proper use for this locally well-loved house, and the situation was exacerbated by damage done by troops billeted there during the war. So, in November 1964, it was unceremoniously destroyed, leaving only the reduced stable block and orangery.

1964   From 1962 the south side of Victoria Street, a hotch-potch of randomly adapted Georgian buildings welded together in the 1920s by the Ranby family to form a department store, was systematically demolished, to be replaced by a purpose-built store which can be acclaimed a success, visually at least. At the far end of the range can be seen the Presbyterian (now United Reform) Chapel which replaced T.C. Hine's 1859 Gothic church on the site, the fourth chapel there since 1782. Ranby's later became Debenham's, and the entire block is now the subject of a possible redevelopment scheme. To the left of the traffic bollard is the spot where the children were pictured playing in the 1932 flood (see p. 56); the building to the right is the former Royal Hotel, at the time of this photograph DHSS offices and shops, but elegantly refurbished as a banqueting suite in 1990.

1965   This year saw the death of the founder of modern meteorology, Sir George Clarke Simpson KCB. Born in East Street, Derby, in 1878, he was the second of the three sons of Alderman Arthur Simpson, who served as Mayor of Derby in 1907–8 and came from an old Derby family. George (known universally as 'Sunny Jim') was educated at the Diocesan School, Friar Gate, and Owen's College, Manchester. By 1915 he was DSc and FRS, having served with distinction as the meteorologist on Captain Scott's ill-fated Antarctic expedition of 1911–12, during which he lost his great friend Lt H.R. Bowers. He was Director of the Meteorological Office from 1920 to 1938 and President of the British Meteorological Society from 1940 to 1942, being knighted in 1935. Unfortunately, Derby has never seen fit to honour this extraordinary man.

1965   The continuing clearance of low-grade nineteenth-century artisans' housing led to the loss of several close-knit communities, their corner shops and taverns. Pictured here, shortly before closure in 1965, is the High Street Tavern in High Street, which despite its name was one of a rather drab series of streets pitched in the 1840s between London Road and Osmaston Road. Their destruction made room for the enormous, much-needed, yet dispiritingly ugly expansion of the Derbyshire Royal Infirmary. The inn was built in 1859.

1966 St Alkmund's Church, established as a minster before the town itself was founded, was last rebuilt, to a particularly elegant design, by H.I. Stevens in 1843, and lay in a Georgian square just off Bridge Gate. Seen here in about 1960, Bridge Gate was pitched from King Street to a new bridge over the Derwent around 1226, along the line of the town's Saxon defensive ditch, apparent in this view. The street contained a rich collection of early, chiefly vernacular, buildings, some of which can be seen beyond the church. In 1966 it was finally cleared of buildings (except the Convent of Mercy, just visible to the extreme left) and drastically excavated to take the line of the inner ring road. This led to the destruction of Derby's only Georgian square, grouped around St Alkmund's Church, although its value was barely apparent to many local people at the time owing to long neglect. *Inset*: The interior.

1963 St Alkmund's vicarage of 1731 by William Trimmer of Derby, altered in 1804 by John Finney, was part of Derby's Georgian Square (see p. 88). Some of the other houses were also very fine indeed, and there were two inns, the Lamb and the late sixteenth-century Eagle and Child, which closed the square off from Queen Street.

1967   The last trains along the GNR line through Derby (Friar Gate) station ran in 1967, leading to the closure and abandonment of the station site. Thirty-three years later it is still untouched by the numerous development plans proposed for it. The fine bridge was eventually bought from British Rail by the city council for £1, and was earmarked to carry the next phase of the inner ring road across Friar Gate, seen here, Derby' premier conservation area. If only the original inner ring road scheme had been harmonised with the closure of the railway, much needless destruction could have been avoided.

1967   The coming of the inner ring road having caused the destruction of the 1861 cattle market, wholesale market and abattoir, new facilities, designed by Borough Architect T. East, were opened on the Meadows, on the east side of the Derwent. This development gathered around it a modest-sized industrial estate, interspersed with motor car concessionaires and Bamford's Auction Rooms. Pictured is East's auction ring, shortly after its inauguration in 1967.

1968 The one silver lining to the unprecedented destruction wrought to the townscape by the inner ring road was that in removing St Alkmund's Church, the opportunity was taken to excavate the site, one of the oldest in the city. Much Saxon and early medieval carved stonework was found, including the vestiges of at least two previous churches and a virtually intact stone sarcophagus, of early ninth-century date, decorated with carved interlace patterning. Here a party from Derby Civic Society visit the excavations in the shell of Stevens' church and listen to the late Dr C.A. Raleigh Radford, the distinguished director of the excavation, expatiating on progress. Part of the sarcophagus – believed to be that of the Eldorman Athelwulf, and now the pride of Derby Museum – is visible, lower left.

1968 Thomas Evans' mill complex at Darley Abbey, pictured a year or two after closure in 1968. The complex was bu
from 1782 on a site formerly occupied by a flint mill, and is one of the finest in the Derwent Valley, if not in the count
and in 2004 they were relisted Grade I and included in the Derwent Valley Mills World Heritage Site. Called the Boar's He
Mills, after the Evans family crest, they were gradually reused as light industrial units,which has ensured their survival. W
the purpose-built mill village, church of 1819 and school of 1824 (both by Moses Wood of Nottingham) in an incompara
setting by the river, the village of Darley Abbey is an impressive and precious survival.

1969 In his ambitious Centra
Improvement Plan, Herbert As
contrived to insert a purpose-
built newspaper kiosk into the
scheme, between the proposed
council chamber and the open
market. However, he neglected
the requirements of those seeki
refreshment 'on the hoof', an
omission repaired during the w
by the erection of this shack
beside the open market, from
which a variety of refreshment
could be obtained when the
market was open. In this view
1969 a few weary bargain-
hunters queue for tea and a
sausage roll. This engaging
facility failed to survive the
closure of the open market in t
early 1980s.

The 1970s

1970   The demise of the last of Derby's street markets came early in the year with the loss of Cockpit Hill market, long a haunt of larger-than-life characters such as 'Roarin' Harry' and 'Feeble Len'. This picture was taken in 1965, and shows the market in full swing, with the bus station behind, and the vast bulk of the Council House forming a backdrop.

1970 The market was closed – inevitably – for redevelopment, in this case the systematic eradication of all the early Regency streets between Albion Street (see p. 59) and Traffic Street (see p. 74) and east of St Peter's Street. In 1970 work began in earnest on the much-trumpeted Eagle Centre, a shopping centre of outstanding hideousness outside and labyrinthine complexity within. But once again, the opportunity was taken to indulge in archaeology, under the supervision of the late R.G. Hughes of the Museum aided by Mr Peter Brady of Little Eaton. They hoped to recover wasters and other evidence of the 1750–79 Cockpit Hill Pot Works and, if possible, to try to detect traces of Derby's shadowy twelfth-century adulterine castle. Note the dome of Alexander MacPherson's 1913 Co-op store in the background and, half-hidden behind a lamp standard, the neon-lit 1930s 'Co-op Cow' logo, much loved locally, and saved from a developer in 2000.

1971 Full Street: Derby's former Municipal Power Station, pictured in the year of its demise. The first phase of 1892 was built nearby in Sowter Road. On this site work began in 1904, under borough architect John Ward, and was completed (as seen here) by Arthur and George Eaton in 1927.

1971 One famous Derby firm moved out of the town centre in this year. Davis & Son (Derby) Ltd was founded by John Davis (1810–73) in 1832 to make scientific instruments in Iron Gate. When, in 1870, the firm moved to the corner of Amen Alley – seen here during the works' demolition – it caused the destruction of the medieval Bath Inn. In 1971 Davis & Son moved out to Nottingham Road. Unfortunately the site – a crucially important one, being separated only by this medieval side road from the east end of the Cathedral – has remained empty ever since, two highly invidious schemes having been seen off in the meantime. A current, and acceptable, scheme still awaits building.

1972 Derelict properties at the east end of Albert Street, opposite the Corn Exchange. The New Market Vaults (built to designs by G.H. Sheffield as the Star Vaults in 1869, and later known as the Albert Vaults, complete with music hall) were closed in 1971 and demolished in the spring of 1972. The area was subsequently landscaped to improve the Albert Street–Morledge junction. Note Sam Adams tripe shop (see p. 44).

1972 The north side of the Market Place is being cleared to make way for Sir Hugh Casson's monolithic new Assembly Room. A further archaeological dig took place, in the process telling us that the Market Place area was not settled earlier than 1100 The seventeenth-century town house of the Cavendish Dukes of Newcastle (which, of course, should never have been demolishe in the first place) was found to have a fifteenth-century timber-framed burgess house attached to the rear, which had remained a service quarters. This was recorded and removed for re-erection beside the Industrial Museum, a scheme which fell victim t 'cuts' in 1981. The museum, ordered to dispose of the parts, gave them to a developer for re-erection in a yard off Sadler Gat although planning niceties forced it to be re-erected without the ground floor!

1972 By the summer of 1972 it was learned that Messrs Casson & Conder, architects of the new Assembl Rooms, wanted no part of the council's scheme to incorporate the façade of the old Assembly Rooms into their building, and the council gave way. It is seen here in the August, scaffolded ready for dismantling for dispatch to Crich Tramway Museum, where it now stands, albeit looking a trifle incongruous!

1972 The Royal School for the Deaf was founded by Dr William Roe (1843–1920) as the Derby Deaf and Dumb Institution in 1874. This energetic and far-sighted man was able to obtain royal patronage in 1890, and acquired sufficient funds to erect a dedicated building, finished to designs by R. Ernest Ryley in 1894 in Friar Gate, immediately west of Friar Gate railway station, and seen here when new (the plane trees, planted in the 1870s, grew too quickly to allow a satisfactory photograph at any later date). The box by the street lamp, left foreground, is still there, and was part of the equipment relating to the installation of electric street lights in 1893. In 1972 the school moved to a site along Ashbourne Road, and this colossal edifice was destroyed, to be replaced by a rather dull housing complex.

1973 Little Chester, a mile north of the city centre on the east bank of the Derwent, has its origins in the Saxon village which grew up around the vestiges of Roman *Derventio*. It was given to the College of All Saints' when Derby was founded to provide the canons with income, each having a farm or prebend in the township. The sub-Dean enjoyed the most opulent, Stone House Prebend, seen here after having been damaged by arsonists while lying empty in 1973. It is Derby's oldest domestic property, part going back to the fourteenth century, and with a fine panelled Jacobean drawing room. Given to the borough by Queen Mary I, only three of these farms remained in 1900. One was demolished in 1964 but the others were rescued, this one being acquired by sympathetic owners who gradually restored it.

1974 After the loss of the Royal School for the Deaf in 1972, it seemed that no further damage could be done to a street as elegant as Friar Gate. Yet in 1974 Derby's earliest Nonconformist chapel – the Presbyterian Meeting House of 1694 beside The Friary – was demolished, along with the adjacent County Club of 1795, to build a colossal development ironically called 'Heritage Gate' and built over-scale in relation to the street in feeble mock-Georgian. Even today, thirty-two years later, parts of it have never been let. The chapel had been transferred to the Unitarians, with the persuasion of the Strutts, in the late eighteenth century, and remained as one of the most important buildings of its type in the region. It is seen here in July 1974 awaiting its fate.

1976 The transformation of Cockpit Hill was complete by this time, and the Eagle Centre opened, seen here from the bus station, with which it connected by a much-vandalised glass and steel bridge (not shown). The Castle and Falcon replaced an inn of the same name which occupied the same site from 1818 to 1971; it is not an improvement. East Street is visible all the way to St Peter's Street, far right.

1976 The Albion Street entrance was hardly artfully contrived, and the Co-op's store, left, with its channelled steel finish, makes for a stark and unwelcoming effect, exacerbated by the surrounding walls of brick and concrete. Happily, this aspect was vastly improved in 1993 with buildings of some quality.

1976 The focus of the interior was Copecastle Square, adorned with a rectangular digital clock dial supported on a piece of what the council fondly believed was 'modern art', but which most people considered was something knocked up in Smith's clock works by apprentices with a pile of redundant packing cases! It lasted barely a decade before vanishing. The entire complex was swept away and replaced by Westfield shoppimgtowns in 2007.

1976   Such was the pressure for new housing that the grounds of older houses began to be infilled – even single dwellings in the gardens of Edwardian houses – leading eventually, in 1999, to the building of estates over the park of Highfields, a minor country house on the edge of Darley Abbey. This picture is of another Highfields, off Duffield Road, built by the ubiquitous Alderman Leaper in 1822 for the Revd Edward Unwin, a grandee with an estate in Staffordshire, and vicar of St Werburgh. This Highfields was sold by its proprietor, a retired estate agent, shorn of its pleasure grounds, upon which these unappealing (but no doubt comfortable) maisonettes were built, seen here newly completed on 6 December 1976. In development terms it is typical of the later twentieth century, but it could all have been done so much better.

1978   The destruction wrought by the demand for housing continued. This is Allestree Fields Farm, a superb estate farmhouse from a design by James Wyatt, who built the nearby Hall (still surviving in council ownership, albeit gutted by drastic treatment for dry rot) for Bache Thornhill of Stanton-in-Peak in 1802. Its demesne, lying between the A6 at Darley Abbey and the Derwent by Little Eaton, was acquired by Bovis Homes for new housing, and the farmhouse was used as a site office, as shown here on 4 November. But this handsome and usefully compact building, which could so easily have been adapted, with its outbuildings, as delightful dwellings, was unceremoniously removed once the new houses were complete. This had happened to the larger but similar Home Farm a few years before.

1978   The decision by the City Council (as it now was) to convert part of the former Derby racecourse into an additional football pitch led the museum staff to mount a rescue excavation on the site, it being known that the northern end of the racecourse was a potential Roman site. Forced on site in a particularly cold November were most of the available staff – not just the two trained archaeologists but natural historians, art curators, industrial experts, even clerks. The site was eventually handed over to a team of professionals, and a series of plinth tombs was found flanking the (Roman) road to the east like a miniature Appian Way, along with a fine columbarium, thus establishing that Roman *Derventio* was a more important settlement than previously suspected. Here two press-ganged amateurs are at work on the base of a plinth-tomb.

1979 According to John Speed's 1610 map of Derby, a medieval cross, lacking its shaft, then stood at the western extremity of Friar Gate. It was called, naturally enough, the Headless Cross. When the beast markets were moved from this part of Friar Gate to the cattle market in 1861, this venerable landmark was shifted to the arboretum. It was repatriated to approximately its original position at the suggestion of the Conservation Area Advisory Committee in June 1979. The inauguration, seen here, was a very low-key affair, with a handful of the Committee members present, along with the late George Rennie (1946–99), Chief Urban Designer, extreme right, whose idea it was. The 'Launderama' (left, background) provides a nice period touch.

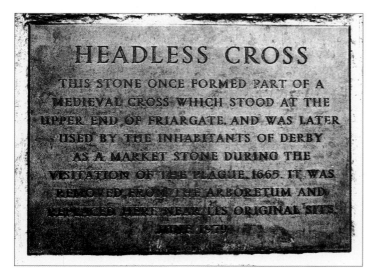

1979 This plaque was attached to the repositioned Headless Cross. It alludes to the plague, when the hollow in the top of the cross was filled with vinegar as a crude form of disinfectant, and payments placed within. This was probably the severe outbreak in Derby of 1637, not that of 1665, when only Eyam suffered at all severely.

102

The Last Decades

1980   The Midland Railway Servants' Orphanage was a magnificent French chateau-style pile set on rising ground just south of the Ashbourne Road, and was built in 1882–7 to designs by A.A. Langley and Edward Fryer of Derby. By all accounts it was as grim within as without until it was utterly transformed by Miss Seaver from 1948. It was replaced by more modern accommodation in 1977, and the old building was demolished in 1980. In 1993 the institution closed completely, to be replaced by a vast new hall of residence for the University of Derby.

1984 Derby's only twin city is Osnabrück in Germany, and the union was struck in 1976, 316 years after the latter was the birthplace of George I. The year 1984 saw the inauguration of Osnabrück Square, between Albert Street and the Market Hall (refurbished five years later) in which was erected a small stone obelisk, presented by the German city, seen here in a photograph of July 1992 coyly hiding behind a tactlessly positioned waste bin. The range to the left was built at the same time to replace the reused shell of Derby's first bus station, made redundant in 1933. To the right can be seen part of one of the vending kiosks built on the square. *Inset*: The same area in 1973 shows a considerable contrast. The fish market of 1926 (see p. 47) had yet to be removed, and the old vending kiosks left much to be desired. Nevertheless the one nearest the camera was a century-old converted cabbies' rest, and strenuous but unsuccessful attempts were made to preserve it (although not necessarily *in situ*). Behind is the great blank brick cliff of the rear elevation of Littlewood's, Cornmarket, built in 1969.

1986 The contraction in Nonconformist congregations continued apace, leading to the demolition of a number of chapels. This photograph, taken on 16 February, has a hint of divine retribution about it, however. The Wesleyan chapel of 1878 – designed by John Wills of Derby, who was responsible for over one hundred chapels of this denomination nationwide – was closed in the early 1980s, but Messrs Stansfield, the demolition contractors, forgot to ask if there was a crypt; there was, as the JCB driver found out on this cold grey Sunday morning!

1988 Built around an impressive *cour d'Honneur* at various dates between 1660 and 1828, the old Shire Hall complex included courts, prisoners' accommodation, judges' lodgings and a former inn, comprising the finest Classical legal complex surviving intact in the Midlands, possibly excepting Lincoln Castle. With the loss of the Crown courts in 1988, the building was commandeered by the Bench, and a seriously damaging plan was drawn up to convert the buildings for magistrates' use. Unfortunately, more space was needed than this Grade I listed complex could accommodate, and over one-third of it was earmarked for demolition. After a vehement battle led by Derby Civic Society, the plans were shelved pending a private finance initiative. A much less damaging scheme was completed in 2004.

1988   In 1982 Derby Museum purchased a fine Grade I
listed house in Friar Gate which had been built in 1769 by
the architect Joseph Pickford (1734–82) for himself. The
City Council made some serious errors in the restoration,
but it opened as a museum in the autumn of 1988, and
has since been much improved, both in its collections and
overall quality.

1989   In 1982 St Werburgh's Church, a foundation that
pre-dates the establishment of Derby itself, was closed by the
diocese, despite a large and enthusiastic congregation built
up by a charismatic parson. The parish was amalgamated
with St Alkmund's, and Sir Arthur Blomfield's impressive
1894 church was sold to a developer. It is seen here
undergoing rebuilding for its new role in August. The
development had failed within five years, and a new role as
a Chinese restaurant was finally agreed in 2004. The 1699
chancel – where Dr Johnson was married in 1735 –
remains with the Redundant Churches Fund.

1990 One of two vast office blocks, completed in 1872–3, built side by side on Nelson Street adjacent to the station and designed by Midland Railway's architect, J.H. Saunders. The one nearest the camera was the accounts offices, the further one the goods offices. A campaign by Derby Civic Society saved the buildings from being destroyed to make a car park. Seen here prior to sensitive restoration and combination as Midland House – HQ of Midland Main Line – by Derek Latham & Associates of Derby in 1992. The colossal scale and generous room height proved ideal for the installation of computer ducting and air conditioning.

1992 Starting in 1990 the City Council initiated the 'Derby Promenade', a scheme which involved pedestrianising the whole north–south axis through the city from the Cathedral to the Spot, embellished with brightly painted faux Victorian street furniture, a monument to Joseph Wright ARA, an interesting decorative iron screen across the lower end of Cornmarket and a fountain. The scheme overall may be counted a success, but few had a good word for the fountain (officially a 'water feature'), a very eclectic affair by Walter Pye, with overtones of the Maginot Line. Nevertheless, young children love its interactive aspects in summer, and it has provided the excuse for an annual Cathedral well-dressing, initiated, as seen here in 1997, by the bishop. Behind is the monumental bulk of part of the 1977 Assembly Rooms.

1992 Derby was selected as the site for one of fifteen City Techology Colleges as part of a government initiative, and the Landau Forte College – its name reflecting those of its principal sponsors – was opened in 1992. It takes a range of pupils of all abilities from primary schools within the city and has had unparallelled success with almost all of its intake; its results have improved year on year. In 2007 it was agreed the school should convert to being one of the new City Academies. The school was built on part of the site of the original Derby china factory.

108

1993 Thanks to lobbying by the Derby Civic Society, the City Council designated Duffield Road and Strutt's Park a Conservation Area, with the aim of preventing infill in the grounds of the numerous large villas on the west side, mainly in public ownership. One of the best, Parkfields, had been adapted in the 1920s as a maternity hospital, which closed in 1992. Instead of pulling down the hospital extension, the entire site was cleared for a small group of 'executive homes'. One interesting feature of the former gardens was the urn, pictured here in February 1993, which has been identified as one of those from the parapet of the 1731 Guildhall. It was suffered to remain as a feature on site.

1994   The Eagle Centre had been a problem since building, especially the market area, provided to replace the old open market. The layout was chaotic, with hexagonal stalls, narrow meandering aisles and no obvious through route. It was closed for rebuilding after a change of council control, and reopened in 1994. This is the view from inside looking out in February 1995, taken from a point almost exactly opposite the photograph on p. 99 – a notable contrast.

1994   Within, the transformation was equally apparent. Despite a rather industrial appearance, the environment is light and airy, the aisles wide and laid out in a grid with a central square, with sensibly shaped, lockable stalls, as here. At the time of writing, work has begun on a scheme to improve and vastly extend the rest which is at present claustrophobic, airless and confusingly laid out.

1994   The university's atrium opened in 1994, a fine and engaging space incorporating a grand entrance which subtly united the hotch-potch of 1950s and '60s tower blocks erected on a very prominent site between Allestree and Markeaton. The university was then but two years old, having been unexpectedly elevated from its former status as a Technical College in 1992 (since the 1970s incorporating the former Teacher Training College). The vast increase in numbers of students has transformed the west side of Derby with five new halls of residence – all frighteningly monolithic and dull buildings – and a huge burgeoning of places of entertainment, often bringing into use interesting historic buildings, but rather at the expense of retailing.

1995   The 250th anniversary of the 'Forty-Five' was celebrated by the installation of a bronze equestrian statue of Bonnie Prince Charlie, whose romantic but ill-starred attempt to restore the legitimate ruling dynasty reached as far as Derby, where he was persuaded to abandon his march on the capital – the only time Derby has ever played a pivotal role in great historical events. The statue, supported by an appeal, and first suggested by the writer in 1988, was the gift of local philanthropist Lionel Pickering to a rather grudging City Council. The first equestrian statue to be erected anywhere in Britain since the war, it is by Anthony Stones and was unveiled in Full Street opposite the Cathedral on the exact anniversary.

1996 This year saw the listing of two Victorian churches in Normanton – St Thomas and St James, both by Joseph Peacock (1821–93) – and the demolition of a third, St Chad, the pleasingly intimate chancel of which is seen here in 199 when it closed. Much use was made of local alabaster, mined at Chellaston, and the stained glass was of a high standard Designed by H. Turner of London and built in 1882, it had fallen into poor repair through neglect, and the intention was t demolish the church, sell part of the site for development, and build afresh, smaller and simpler. Sadly, the site is still empty no successor is in sight and the dwindling congregation has to make do with temporary accommodation. An appeal, repa and regular maintenance would have been the better option.

1997 A scheme was initiated in this year to re-use the historic No. 1 Engine Roundhouse (by Francis Thompson, 1840) along with the attached Old Works Offices and clock tower and the nearby Midland Counties Railway workshops of 1839, these having come within the ambit of the Pride Park special development area in 1995 and been upgraded, after a long battle, to Grade II*. Demolition of the works complex began with the end of the steam age, continued under British Rail Engineering Ltd and their successors. Here a party from the Civic Society views the matchless roof of the roundhouse. The site was finally acquired for conversion into new premises for Derby College in 2007.

997 Derby County FC was a founding member of the League, and moved from the Cricket Ground to the Baseball Ground
1895. The latter was a manifestation of an enthusiasm for the US game developed by industrialist Sir Francis Ley Bt, who
id it out next to his foundry, and started a baseball league, which lasted from 1890 to 1898. Soccer then filled the vacuum,
d Derby County went on to win the FA Cup in 1946, and the League Championship in 1972 and 1975. Here a match is
progress in 1954, with Ley's factory in the background.

After much hesitation, Derby County moved to Pride Park and a new stadium was built to modern hi-tech designs.
is move proved to be the catalyst that enabled the entire site to 'take off' in economic terms, and after years of uncertainty
has proved a successful exercise in urban regeneration. The site of the old Baseball ground was redeveloped for housing
m 2007.

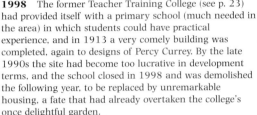

1998   The former Teacher Training College (see p. 23) had provided itself with a primary school (much needed in the area) in which students could have practical experience, and in 1913 a very comely building was completed, again to designs of Percy Currey. By the late 1990s the site had become too lucrative in development terms, and the school closed in 1998 and was demolished the following year, to be replaced by unremarkable housing, a fate that had already overtaken the college's once delightful garden.

1999   With the regaining of unitary status by the city in 1996, it was no longer in thrall to the County Council for road and plans were published to complete the inner ring road, stalled since 1974. One of the most threatened places is Kin Street, the main route north, which is constricted and edged with listed buildings. One building which is unique in the UK the former spar works of Richard Brown & Co., built in 1802 on the site of Old St Helen's House. Here worked Matthe Bolton's only serious rival in the production of Blue John ornaments and other *objets de vertu*. The showroom can be see nearest the camera, with Brown's house behind and the (modified) workshop beyond. Behind again was the steam engir house of 1802 and, oddly, a swimming pool open to the public for a small payment, which opened in 1823 and closed i 1852. The firm lasted through two subsequent ownerships until it became the victim of dwindling orders for war memoria and the Great Depression. It is the only surviving spar manufactory of this date anywhere; its survival will be a test o Derby's respect for its heritage as it enters the twenty-first century.

1999 John Whitehurst FRS (1813–88) – co-founder of the Lunar Society, clockmaker, scientist and founder of modern geological science – was one of the truly great men associated with Derby. His friend Joseph Pickford rebuilt for him a fine house in Queen Street, once the home of the first Astronomer Royal John Flamsteed FRS (1646–1719). Joseph Wright also died here in 1797, and by coincidence it was, for 149 years, the offices of John Smith & Sons, clockmakers, a company founded by a former employee of John Whitehurst. Before Smiths moved out in 1999, it was adorned with a rare angle barometer by Whitehurst, and by Wright's portrait of the great man, both visible in this photograph. If ever there was a shrine to Derby's finest hour, this room is it. Twice refused statutory listing, the building is to be retained as part of a large complex of apartments.

1999 Another positive step, albeit a minor one, was the installation over the Markeaton Brook of a near-replica of the [Re]gency footbridge that had been destroyed by the council in 1977 as unsafe, and once a visual paradigm of the old West End. [W]hen the university built Sir Peter Hilton House – a hall of residence named after a well-loved Lord Lieutenant (1978–94) who [die]d in 1995 – on a former mill site by the brook, the City Council's urban designer suggested that the bridge be reinstated as a *[quid] pro quo*. An engineer then produced a design closely based on the original. The result is most gratifying.

1999 The Cockpit Hill multi-storey car park (see p. 76) is so monolithic that this charming view down the Derwent from the silk mill is no longer able to be enjoyed. Almost the whole of the patch of sky above Exeter Bridge is obscured by this uniquely obtrusive edifice. Note the elegant river frontage of Aslin's magistrates' courts and police station to the right (both due for closure but recently spot-listed Grade II); would that subsequent developments on the opposite bank in the 1980s had shown such respect for the view from the river!

1999 The university proposed a multi-faith centre – something so far unique – to be built on their campus in Kedleston Road, and came up with a splendidly organic design, seen here as envisaged. It is hoped to begin work in 2001 and that the finished building will generally raise local architectural standards markedly. It was completed to a revised design in 2005.

2000 In June came the announcement that the 124-year-old firm of Royal Crown Derby had regained its independence from a large conglomerate for the first time for very many years. This development was all the more fitting as the year also marked the 250th anniversary of porcelain manufacture in the city. Seen here is an exceptionally fine RCD campana urn, almost a foot in height, made in 1903, and decorated by William Edwin Mosley, one of the finest china painters of that era.

117

1901 View from St Alkmund's Church Yard across Bridge Gate to the Catholic Church of St Mary, designed by A.W.N. Pugin in 1838–44, and extended by his son, E.W. Pugin. To the right is the west front of St Alkmund's, by Henry Isaac Stevens, 1843, on the site of Derby's oldest minster church. To the left, the Regency Golden Lion inn. Bridge Gate, named after the crest of the Earls of Shrewsbury (St Mary's having been largely subsidised by the sixteenth Earl) and closed in 1908.

2000 The same view subsequent to the building of the inner ring road in 1967–8. St Alkmund's, its largely Georgian Square and the Golden Lion have all gone. A wind-buffeted footbridge connects the surviving stub-end of Bridge Gate, left of the church, to a footpath which climbs from an underpass connecting with Queen Street through a non-descript piece of scrubland covered in cotoneaster and litter, and surrounded by a whirligig of roads.

2000 A corner of Derby County Football Club's 'Hi-tech' new stand in Pride Park, looking towards the site of the railway works. The shop caters for the ever-loyal fans of 'The Rams', a name derived from the legendary Derby Ram of local song and fable. The club was one of the founders of the football league and is currently making its way in the Premiership.

Acknowledgements and Picture Credits

owe heartfelt thanks to a good number of people who have supplied help and information for the reparation of this book, not least of whom are the ever-helpful staff of the Derby Local Studies brary, my former colleagues at Derby Museum and very many friends. Furthermore, I am indebted a number of people at the *Derby Evening Telegraph*, especially the library staff there, and to merous readers of my column in that newpaper, who have written in at various times to correct d expand my knowledge of Derby. From Derby City Council I have had years of friendly assistance om the late George Rennie, Chief Urban Designer, his colleagues and successors, to all of whom I am ateful. Finally, I owe a great deal to my wife Carole for her continuing help, suggestions and support, r which I am especially grateful.

Photographs have been willingly lent by a number of sources. In addition to my own collection, I ave been able to draw on the collections of James Darwin and Derby Museum, and another splendid llection whose owner wished to remain anonymous; from these four sources have come the bulk of e pictures used. I am also grateful to M. Allseybrook Esq., J.E. Behrendt Esq., the late Revd Derek ckley, the late Mrs A.R. Carter, Alan Champion Esq., *Derbyshire Life*, Don Farnsworth Esq., Tony iffin Esq., the late Roy Hughes (courtesy of his widow Betty), Mrs P. Lander, Mrs E. Lewin, the late rs W. Moore, Neale's, Mrs R. Patrick, the late George Rennie, the University of Derby, and B. Walton q. To each and every one of these kind people I am extremely grateful, especially for their illingness to make their photographs available to me.

It is worth pointing out that there are three main public collections of Derby photographs, those of rby Local Studies Library (well over 1,000), the National Monuments Record, Swindon (several ndreds), and the 13,000 plus (all copied on to negative) at Derby Museum. The *Derby Evening legraph* library also has several thousand prints which, while not strictly speaking a public collection, n be made available at a modest charge. People with unwanted pictures on their hands, or with llections to dispose of, should think seriously about donating them in the first instance to Derby useum, The Strand, Derby, DE1 1BS.

axwell Craven was born in London in 1945, and was with Derby Museum for twenty five years, om 1982 to 1998 (when made compulsorily redundant) as Keeper of Antiquities. Since 1979 he has ritten fourteen books, mainly on Derby and Derbyshire subjects, including *The Derbyshire Country ouse* (with Michael Stanley, 1991), *A Derbyshire Armory* (1991), biographies of the photographer chard Keene (1994) and the eighteenth-century scientist and horologer John Whitehurst, FRS 996), as well as contributing numerous articles to both local and national periodicals and agazines. He is married, with a daughter, and living in Derby, where he writes a column for the rby Evening Telegraph*, conservation briefs, and researches for the auctioneers Bamfords of Derby. He ceived an honorary degree from the new University of Derby in 1996 and was made MBE and ected FSA in 1999.

121